Precision Navigation: A Key Component for a Connected World

Navya

Contents

Chapter 1

Introduction

Accurate, reliable and fast localization has never been more important. Autonomous driving and advanced driving assistance systems require that vehicles can locate themselves in all types of environments and weather. Another application is the Internet of Things, where a vast amount of objects need to be connected and localized. Location-based services in, e.g., smartphones need regular updates on the user's position. In indoor areas, localization can be done through, e.g., Wi-Fi fingerprinting, however this is an active research field [KH07, p. 89 8]. In outdoor areas, on the other hand, Global Navigation Satellite System (GNSS) is the dominant technology, with almost world-wide availability. Furthermore, GNSS gives an absolute position (relative to the earth), which can be acquired within a matter of seconds after starting the receiver. Drawbacks of GNSS include its high power consumption at high sampling rates and its sensitivity to jamming and spoofing. Another problem, that is especially serious for automotive applications, are the tall buildings in dense urban areas, which reflect and block the signals on their way from satellite to receiver. An example of this from the City of London (latitude 51.510537° and longitude -0.091505°) can be seen at Fig. 1.1, where the receiver position is estimated to be outside the roads for most of the time. Other difficult scenarios are tunnels and indoor parkings. To combat this, GNSS receivers can be combined with other sensors, typically an Inertial Measurement Unit (IMU) that acts in a complementary way by providing relative positioning at a high sampling rate, and it is insensitive to reflections. Furthermore, other wireless ranging signals can be added to aid the GNSS positioning. Sensor fusion of GNSS with IMU and wireless signals are both considered and studied in this book to quantify their relative contributions to reduce positioning errors. However, the focus of this book is GNSS multi-frequency reception, and how it can reduce positioning errors in urban areas. GNSS multi-frequency reception means that the satellites transmit the signals on several carrier frequencies (typically two or three), and that the receiver can process the signals at at least two of these carrier frequencies. As of 2020, this type of receiver is reaching the mass market, mainly in the smartphone market to start with, but it is also a highly interesting option for the automotive mass market.

Figure 1.1: Satellite navigation in dense urban areas can be especially difficult, such as in the City of London [Goo15]. The vehicle was driving along the east-west road in the middle of the figure, however the navigation system estimated positions of up to 50 m north of that road, due to tall buildings blocking and reflecting the satellite signals.

> The section for related work in this chapter is primarily based on [OBB18], with the addition of more recent works.

1.1 Research Questions

The goal of the research presented in this book is to improve the accuracy of positioning in urban areas with the help of multi-frequency GNSS transmission. The research questions are

- Which statistical distribution do the pseudorange errors caused by reflections in urban follow? How do pseudoranges on two carrier frequencies differ?

- How can multi-frequency reception be used to classify the reception mode of the received signal from a satellite? Which observables are relevant for this?

- Are there multi-frequency-based methods to mitigate errors caused by reflections, i.e., to repair the faulty measurements so they are still useful?

- To which extent can the multi-frequency-based methods contribute to reducing positioning errors in urban areas, compared with sensor fusion approaches?

1.2   Basics of Satellite Navigation

Since the United States launched the first Global Positioning System (GPS) [Glo15] satellite in 1978, other satellite navigation systems with global reach have been developed. These include the Russian Globalnaya Navigatsionnaya Sputnikovaya Sistema (GLONASS) [Rus17], the Galileo [Eur16] of the European Union, and the Chinese BeiDou Navigation Satellite System (BDS) [Chi17]. The methods presented in this book are mainly based on GPS, because at the time of data collection GPS had the most number of satellites available for dual-frequency transmission. The simulation-based results also partly include the Galileo system, which is similar to GPS, with the exception of the modulation schemes of several signals.

GNSS Segments   Satellite navigation systems typically consist of three segments: a space segment, a control segment, and a user segment. The space segment are the satellites, which orbit earth and transmit signals containing information about their identity, position, and status. The control segment is a network of stations on the ground; GPS has two master control stations, four stations for uploading data to the satellites and 16 stations to monitor the satellites, spread across the earth. The final segment is the user segment, which is the ensemble of all receivers that can process satellite navigation signals, e.g., in smartphones or in vehicular navigation systems.

Orbits and Satellites   Fig. 1.2 shows an example of a receiver that receives 11 GPS satellites. The satellite trajectories are visualized, each one is defined by an inclination (the angle with respect to the earth's equator, which is around $55°$ for all satellites). Moreover, the right ascension of ascending nodes of the orbital planes are $60°$ apart, defining six planes around the globe. Several satellites share these two parameters, however they are then spaced apart in the same orbital plane. Other satellite navigation systems follow similar rules, however, e.g., BDS also uses geostationary orbits. Note that orbital planes are only true in earth-centered inertial coordinate systems, while the rest of this book uses Earth-Centered, Earth-Fixed (ECEF) coordinates.

Channel Access Methods   In GNSS, there are two techniques to distinguish satellites from each other: Code Division Multiple Access (CDMA) [Tor15] and Frequency Division Multiple Access (FDMA). CDMA is the most common one, also known from, e.g., cellular systems. It is used by GPS, Galileo and BDS, where each satellite is given a unique code. This code is a sequence of bits, that can be generated from, e.g., a Gold code [KH07, p. 17]. This is the case for GPS, where each satellite of the L1 Coarse Acquisition (CA) signal is represented by a Gold sequence of 1023 bits. The cross correlation of the code between different satellites is low, to avoid misidentification of the satellites. Historically GLONASS is the only satellite navigation system that used only FDMA, which means that the satellites are distinguished by different carrier frequencies, spaced 0.5625 MHz apart. As of 2020, GLONASS is transmitting both CDMA and FDMA signals.

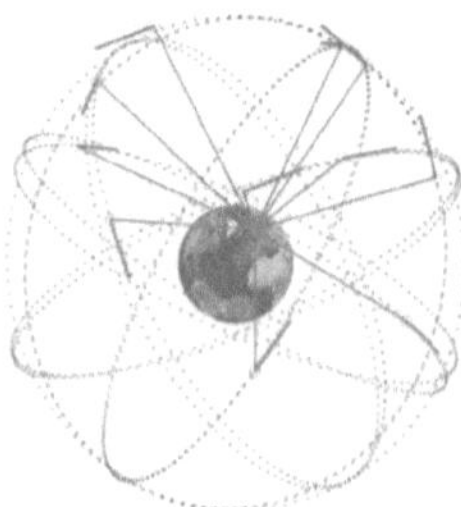

Figure 1.2: At the receiver's location, it can receive all 11 Global Positioning System (GPS) satellites that are above the 10 degree elevation. The satellite orbits are marked in black, and their velocity vectors can be seen as red arrows. The magenta lines represent the line of sight between each satellite and the receiver.

Carrier Frequencies   Different carrier frequencies are not only used for FDMA, most satellite navigation systems use multiple carrier frequencies to transmit several signals. Multi-frequency transmission is a central theme for this book, and Fig. 1.3 gives an overview of the frequency bands used by GPS, GLONASS, and Galileo. Note that the GPS L1 and Galileo E1 signals share a central frequency; the same applies to the GPS L2 and Galileo E5b signals. Dual-frequency signal processing methods can thus be applicable to both systems in many cases.

Modulation Schemes   A central property of a GNSS signal is its modulation scheme, which specifies how the signal encodes the information it contains. This information is the aforementioned ranging code and the navigation data message that contains information about the satellite orbit and status. The most basic modulation scheme used in GNSS is Binary Phase Shift Keying (BPSK), where the signal has two phases, spaced π radians apart. Whenever the symbol switches between 0 and 1, the phase also switches, see Fig. 1.4. Another modulation scheme is Binary Offset Carrier (BOC), used by, e.g., the Galileo System. It uses square sub-carriers, partly to split the spectrum into two parts, to assure the interoperability of satellite navigation systems, see Fig. 1.5.

A summary of the modulation methods, carrier frequencies, chip rates, and details on the codes of the most common open GPS and Galileo signals can be found in Table 1.1. BDS will offer three carrier frequencies (B1, B2, B3) [Chi17] and GLONASS will add an L2 signal to the existing L1 one [Rus17]. The chip frequency is important for accurately determining the pseudorange in urban

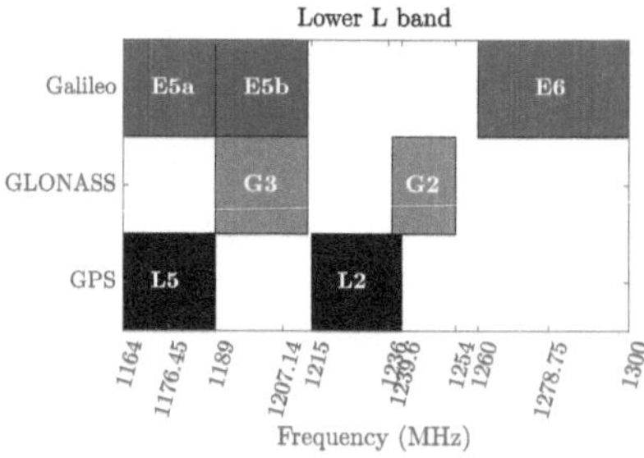

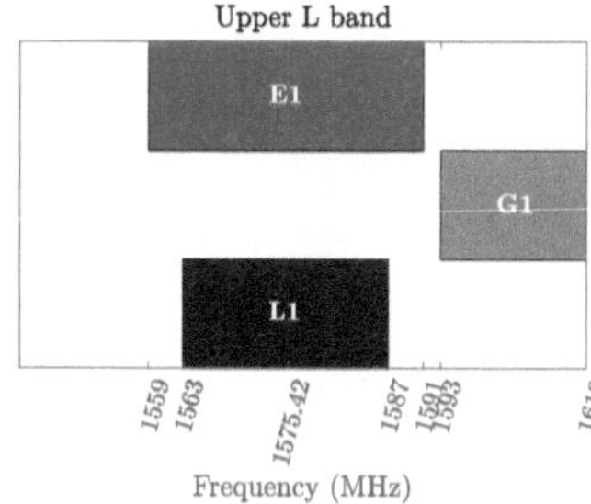

Figure 1.3: The frequency bands of the main signals of Global Positioning System (GPS), Globalnaya Navigatsionnaya Sputnikovaya Sistema (GLONASS), and Galileo are visualized.

Table 1.1: A list of non-restricted signals of GPS and Galileo. The data is based on [Glo15, Glo13, Eur16]. The table is adapted from [OBB18], ©2018 IEEE.

System	Band	Component	f (MHz)	f_{chip} (MHz)	Modulation	Code length (kbits)	Code length (ms)
GPS	L1	CA	1575.42	1.023	BPSK(1)	1.023	1
		C	1575.42	1.023	TMBOC(6,1,4/33)	10.23	10
	L2	CM	1227.6	0.5115	BPSK(1)	10.23	20
		CL	1227.6	0.5115	BPSK(1)	767.25	1500
	L5	SoL	1176.45	10.23	BPSK(10)	10.23	1
Galileo	E1	OS	1575.42	1.023	CBOC(6,1,1/11)	4.092	4
	E5	a	1176.45	10.23	AltBOC(15,10)	10.23	1
		b	1207.14	10.23	AltBOC(15,10)	10.23	1

areas, since a higher one can more easily separate a direct signal from reflections. Many modulation schemes and variants of them exist, in addition to the previously explained BPSK, there is also BOC, Composite Binary Offset Carrier (CBOC), Alternative Binary Offset Carrier (AltBOC) and Time Multiplexed Binary Offset Carrier (TMBOC).

Navigation Message The GPS signal modulates not only a code, on top of this, the so called navigation message is transmitted. The bits of the navigation message are coded by inverting the entire code sequence to send a 0, and by doing nothing to send a 1. For the GPS L1, the navigation message is transmitted at 50 bits per second, and the entire almanac consists of 37.5 kbit (25 sub-pages of 30 seconds, each with 50 bits), so it takes 12.5 minutes to completely decode it, see Fig. 1.6. This time can be reduced by saving the navigation message when the receiver is turned-off (to perform a hot-start later), or by downloading the navigation message via a cellular connection.

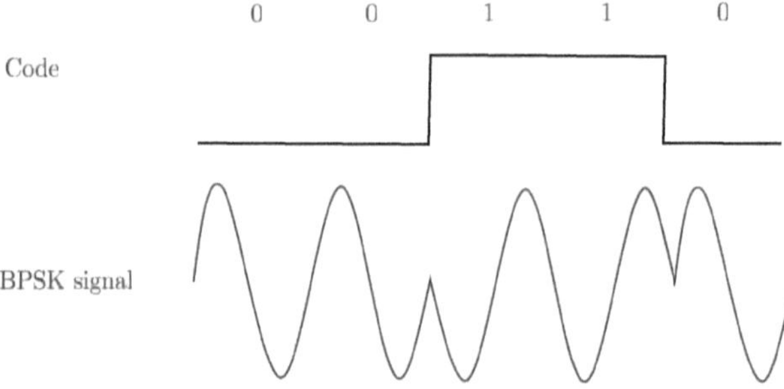

Figure 1.4: In Binary Phase Shift Keying (BPSK), the phase switches between two phases whenever the code changes.

To compute the position, only the ephemeris is necessary, which consists of only two subframes of six seconds. Depending on when the receiver is switched on, this can take between 12 and 36 seconds to decode. The most important part of the navigation message is the information about the satellite positions and trajectories, but it also contains information on their status.

Time-of-Flight Measurement   When arriving at the receiver, the satellite signal is very weak, below the thermal noise floor based on a bandwidth adapted to signal (which is 2 MHz for GPS L1). The CDMA process uses correlation to pick up the signals despite the low signal strength, and as mentioned before, this is also how the satellites are distinguished. Furthermore, the pseudoranges are also computed based on the code correlation. These pseudoranges are the main measurements that a GNSS receiver uses to computes its position. They are one-way measurements of the time-of-flight of from satellite to the receiver. To determine the pseudorange, the correlation between two signals is computed. The first signal is the one that is being received from a satellite, at this point it is unknown which one. The second signal is a replica of the satellite code (the receiver uses one channel per satellite for this). The correlation will be significantly higher for the satellite channel that corresponds to the transmitting satellite. Thereafter, the acquisition of the satellite is done by searching for the correlation peak along several code delay bins and several carrier frequency bins. The search along the code delay will give the time of flight, while the search along the frequency bins will give the Doppler shift, which is related to the satellite and receiver velocities. The satellite acquisition process is visualized in Fig. 1.7, where a Fast Fourier Transform (FFT)-based search has been done. When a signal is acquired, the tracking process keeps computing the code delay and the Doppler shift. While tracking, only the correlation within short delays of the peak (around one chip) that was identified during acquisition needs be computed. One code sequence for the

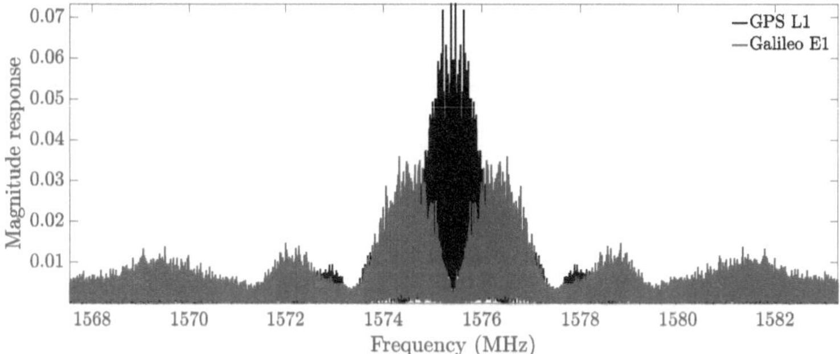

Figure 1.5: The Global Positioning System (GPS) L1 and Galileo E1 signals share a central carrier frequency at 1575.42 MHz, however, the Binary Offset Carrier (BOC) modulation of Galileo improves the interoperability of the two systems.

GPS L1 signal roughly corresponds to 300 km, this creates a code ambiguity to be resolved. This is done by identifying certain frames in the navigation message, which has a significantly larger periodicity than the code. Different tracking methods use different numbers of correlation points, with different spacing in-between them. The tracking is done on two channels, the in-phase and quadrature channels (I and Q), which are separated by a 90° phase difference. For, e.g., the GPS L1 CA signal, the tracking seeks to maximize the energy in the quadrature channel, while keeping the energy in the in-phase channel to a minimum. This, however, differs between different systems and signals.

Navigation Equations The determination of the receiver position r using the pseudorange ρ and the decoded satellite positions s is based on trilateration (or, more general, multilateration). This means solving a non-linear equation system. In this system, one equation per received satellite is given, and four unknown variables need to be estimated: the receiver position in three dimensions, plus the receiver clock bias b. The receiver clock bias is due to the receiver clock not being synchronous to the GPS time. For this reason, b needs has to be treated as an unknown variable in the equation system. Due to this, the position estimation cannot be considered a true multilateration problem. This clock bias actually consists of two parts: one of the receiver (that will be solved along with the equations), and one related to the satellite, which is corrected using information from the navigation message and partly using relativistic clock correction with a second-degree polynomial. The navigation equation system for the minimum number of four

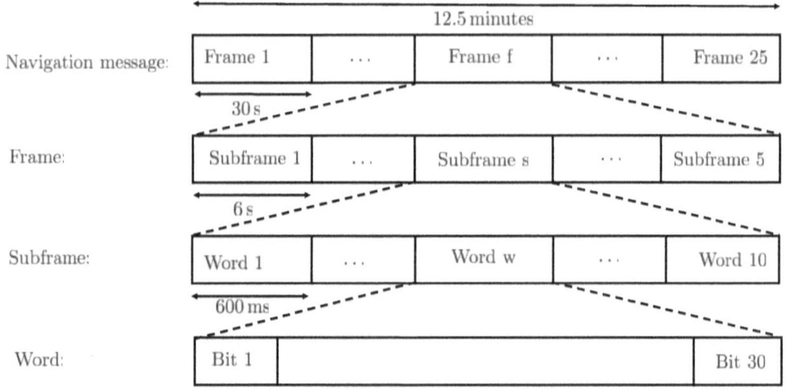

Figure 1.6: The Global Positioning System (GPS) navigation message consists of 25 frames, each made up by 5 subframes. These subframes contain each 10 words, that in turn consist of 30 bits each.

received satellites can be written as

$$
\begin{aligned}
\rho^1 &= \sqrt{(r^x - s^{1,x})^2 + (r^y - s^{1,y})^2 + (r^z - s^{1,z})^2} + b \\
\rho^2 &= \sqrt{(r^x - s^{2,x})^2 + (r^y - s^{2,y})^2 + (r^z - s^{2,z})^2} + b \\
\rho^3 &= \sqrt{(r^x - s^{3,x})^2 + (r^y - s^{3,y})^2 + (r^z - s^{3,z})^2} + b \\
\rho^4 &= \sqrt{(r^x - s^{4,x})^2 + (r^y - s^{4,y})^2 + (r^z - s^{4,z})^2} + b.
\end{aligned}
\tag{1.1}
$$

Closed-Form Solutions Closed-form solutions to the navigation equation system exist [Ban85], including variants that are dedicated to detecting reflection errors [RC09]. These solutions do not generalize for any number of satellites. Furthermore, they are difficult to generalize to include multiple constellations and other sensor measurements.

Gauss-Newton Solution An efficient way of solving non-linear equation systems is the Gauss-Newton (GN) method [Bjö96]. In the case of the system described in (1.1), where the minimum of four satellites are received, the goal is to find a solution to

$$
\begin{aligned}
f_1(x,y,z,b) &= \rho^1 - \sqrt{(r^x - s^{1,x})^2 + (r^y - s^{1,y})^2 + (r^z - s^{1,z})^2} - b = 0 \\
f_2(x,y,z,b) &= \rho^2 - \sqrt{(r^x - s^{2,x})^2 + (r^y - s^{2,y})^2 + (r^z - s^{2,z})^2} - b = 0 \\
f_3(x,y,z,b) &= \rho^3 - \sqrt{(r^x - s^{3,x})^2 + (r^y - s^{3,y})^2 + (r^z - s^{3,z})^2} - b = 0 \\
f_4(x,y,z,b) &= \rho^4 - \sqrt{(r^x - s^{4,x})^2 + (r^y - s^{4,y})^2 + (r^z - s^{4,z})^2} - b = 0.
\end{aligned}
\tag{1.2}
$$

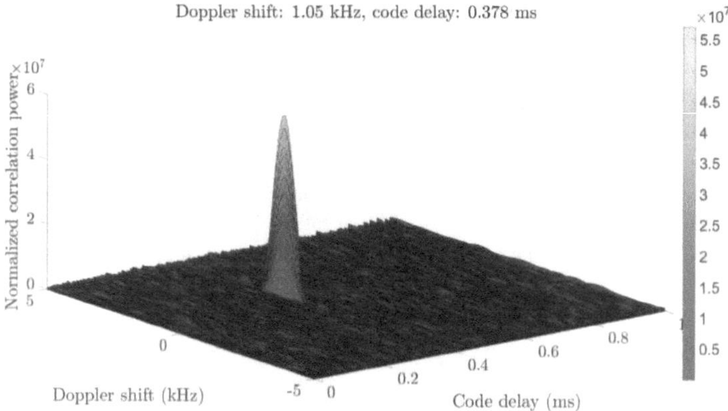

Figure 1.7: To identify the code delay and the Doppler shift of a satellite, a search is made, typically based on Fast Fourier Transform (FFT).

To get closer to the solution, the correction term H needs to be computed, this is the inverse of the Jacobian matrix multiplied with the vector that contains the functions to minimize

$$H = \mathbf{J}^{-1} \begin{bmatrix} f_1(x,y,z,b) & f_2(x,y,z,b) & f_3(x,y,z,b) & f_4(x,y,z,b) \end{bmatrix}^{T} \tag{1.3}$$

The Jacobian matrix is the derivative of each function to minimize in each row, derived with respect to each unknown variable x, y, z, b in each column

$$\mathbf{J} = \begin{bmatrix} \frac{\partial f_1}{\partial x} & \frac{\partial f_1}{\partial y} & \frac{\partial f_1}{\partial z} & \frac{\partial f_1}{\partial b} \\ \frac{\partial f_2}{\partial x} & \frac{\partial f_2}{\partial y} & \frac{\partial f_2}{\partial z} & \frac{\partial f_2}{\partial b} \\ \frac{\partial f_3}{\partial x} & \frac{\partial f_3}{\partial y} & \frac{\partial f_3}{\partial z} & \frac{\partial f_3}{\partial b} \\ \frac{\partial f_4}{\partial x} & \frac{\partial f_4}{\partial y} & \frac{\partial f_4}{\partial z} & \frac{\partial f_4}{\partial b} \end{bmatrix}. \tag{1.4}$$

This process is repeated, subtracting H from the minimization function vector until the norm of H is under a tolerance limit, that has to be selected. The GN method can be sensitive to the initial guess, and if no upper limit in solution time or number of solutions is set, it can get stuck searching for a solution forever. So far, we have ignored pseudorange measurement noise, to which the GN solver is sensitive. This solution is easily generalizable to more than four satellites, and by introducing a new clock bias variable per constellation, multi-constellation variants are also feasible.

Least Squares Solution The Least Squares (LS) [KH07, p. 941] solution exists in two variants: unweighted and weighted. Like the previously explained closed-form and GN solutions, it is a standard method to solve the navigation equations. In this book, the focus is on its version that also incorporates a transition model, the Extended Kalman Filter (EKF), which is explained next.

Extended Kalman Filter Due to its abilities to perform sensor fusion, the EKF is widely used in GNSS. It is a linearized version of the linear Kalman Filter (KF) [Kal60]. The goal is to estimate the state of the receiver, consisting of the 3-dimensional position and clock bias, together with their derivatives with respect to time

$$\mathbf{x}_k = \begin{bmatrix} r_k^x & \dot{r}_k^x & r_k^y & \dot{r}_k^y & r_k^z & \dot{r}_k^z & b_k & \dot{b}_k \end{bmatrix}^T. \tag{1.5}$$

The EKF incorporates a transition model, so information about the movement of the receiver can be incorporated. A common transition model is the Constant Velocity (CV) transition one, supposing that the receiver moves with a constant velocity. It relates the current state to the previous state using the matrix

$$\mathbf{A} = \mathbf{I}_4 \otimes \begin{bmatrix} 1 & \tau \\ 0 & 1 \end{bmatrix}, \tag{1.6}$$

where τ is the sampling interval and $\otimes$ is the Kronecker product [Bro06]. $\mathbf{I}_d$ is an identity matrix of dimension d.

The process covariance matrix for the x, y, and z positions is

$$\mathbf{Q}_{xyz} = \sigma_{xyz}^2 \begin{bmatrix} \frac{\tau^3}{3} & \frac{\tau^2}{2} \\ \frac{\tau^2}{2} & \tau \end{bmatrix}, \tag{1.7}$$

and for the clock and its drift it is

$$\mathbf{Q}_b = \begin{bmatrix} S_f \tau + S_g \frac{\tau^3}{3} & \frac{S_g \tau^2}{2} \\ \frac{S_g \tau^2}{2} & S_g \tau \end{bmatrix}. \tag{1.8}$$

Together, they form the process covariance matrix

$$\mathbf{Q} = \mathrm{diag}\left(\begin{bmatrix} \mathbf{Q}_{xyz} & \mathbf{Q}_{xyz} & \mathbf{Q}_{xyz} & \mathbf{Q}_b \end{bmatrix} \right). \tag{1.9}$$

To create a diagonal matrix with a vector input as its diagonal, the function $\mathrm{diag}(\cdot)$ is used

$$\mathrm{diag}\left(\begin{bmatrix} a_1 & a_2 & a_3 \end{bmatrix} \right) = \begin{bmatrix} a_1 & 0 & 0 \\ 0 & a_2 & 0 \\ 0 & 0 & a_3 \end{bmatrix}. \tag{1.10}$$

The error covariance matrix $\mathbf{P}_k$ is diagonal, with dimension 8×8, and it is initialized according to

$$\mathbf{P}_{k-1} = \mathbf{I}_8 \otimes p_0,$$

(1.11)

where p_0 is a tuning parameter.

Like for the GN solver, an initial estimate of the state, $\hat{\mathbf{x}}_{k-1}^-$ is needed, This choice is important, since the EKF can diverge under certain conditions when the initial state is not well estimated.

When the initial values are set, the EKF starts a loop, where first a prediction of the state

$$\hat{\mathbf{x}}^- = \mathbf{A}\hat{\mathbf{x}}_{k-1}$$

(1.12)

and the error covariance

$$\mathbf{P}_k^- = \mathbf{A}\mathbf{P}_{k-1}\mathbf{A}^T + \mathbf{Q}$$

(1.13)

is made.

Next, supposing that L satellites are received, indexed by l, the linearization via the Jacobian measurement matrix is done

$$\mathbf{J} = \begin{bmatrix} \frac{\partial \rho_1}{\partial x} & 0 & \frac{\partial \rho_1}{\partial y} & 0 & \frac{\partial \rho_1}{\partial z} & 0 & 1 & 0 \\ \vdots & \vdots & \vdots & \vdots & \vdots & \vdots & \vdots & \vdots \\ \frac{\partial \rho_L}{\partial x} & 0 & \frac{\partial \rho_L}{\partial y} & 0 & \frac{\partial \rho_L}{\partial z} & 0 & 1 & 0 \end{bmatrix},$$

(1.14)

where

$$\frac{\partial \rho_l}{\partial x} = \frac{-(s^{l,x} - \hat{r}^x)}{\sqrt{(s^{l,x} - \hat{r}^x)^2 + (s^{l,y} - \hat{r}^y)^2 + (s^{l,z} - \hat{r}^z)^2}}$$

(1.15)

$$\frac{\partial \rho_l}{\partial y} = \frac{-(s^{l,y} - \hat{r}^y)}{\sqrt{(s^{l,x} - \hat{r}^x)^2 + (s^{l,y} - \hat{r}^y)^2 + (s^{l,z} - \hat{r}^z)^2}}$$

(1.16)

$$\frac{\partial \rho_l}{\partial z} = \frac{-(s^{l,z} - \hat{r}^z)}{\sqrt{(s^{l,x} - \hat{r}^x)^2 + (s^{l,y} - \hat{r}^y)^2 + (s^{l,z} - \hat{r}^z)^2}}.$$

(1.17)

The zero columns appear since the derivative of the measurements do not depend on the states containing a time derivative.

The measurement error auto-covariance matrix

$$\mathbf{R} = \mathrm{diag}\left(\begin{bmatrix} \sigma_1^2 & \cdots & \sigma_L^2 \end{bmatrix} \right)$$

(1.18)

is a diagonal matrix with the pseudorange measurement variance along its diagonal.

Then, the Kalman gain

$$\mathbf{K} = \mathbf{P}_k^- \mathbf{J}^T (\mathbf{J}\mathbf{P}_k^- \mathbf{J}^T + \mathbf{R})^{-1}$$

(1.19)

is computed.

The measurement vector consists of the pseudoranges

$$\mathbf{z} = \begin{bmatrix} \rho^1 & \cdots & \rho^L \end{bmatrix}^T. \tag{1.20}$$

Thereafter, the current state estimate is given by

$$\hat{\mathbf{x}}_k = \hat{\mathbf{x}}^- + \mathbf{K}(\mathbf{z} - \mathbf{J}\hat{\mathbf{x}}^-). \tag{1.21}$$

Subsequently, an update of the error covariance matrix is performed

$$\mathbf{P}_k = \mathbf{P}_k^- - \mathbf{K}\mathbf{J}\mathbf{P}_k^-. \tag{1.22}$$

Finally, the EKF processes the next time step by restarting from (1.12). Alternatively, the EKF can be written using the Joseph form for improved performance [BJ68].

Unscented Kalman Filter The Unscented Kalman Filter (UKF) [WV00] is similar to the EKF, however in this case, the linearization is based on the unscented transform, which takes sigma points and passes them through a non-linear function. In this way, a Gaussian distribution is approximated. The UKF has also shown good results in GNSS applications [GHG$^+$18, ZZS$^+$15, LCL$^+$07].

Particle Filter Another method that is widely used for non-linear estimation problems is the particle filter [Del97, LC98]. The position to be estimated is represented by a number of particles, each representing a different position according to a probability density function. The particles are then weighted according to how well their proposed positions fit the measurements. Particle degeneracy, meaning that all particles end up proposing the same position is a problem in particle filters, this can be mitigated by resampling. In order to find a suitable trade-off between computational time and precision, the number of particles has to be well selected. Particle filters have also been successfully applied to GNSS [YLG11].

Single Point Positioning Single Point Positioning (SPP) [KH07, p. 293] is the most standard positioning method in GNSS, it means that the code measurements are used to determine the position. No augmentation services, special corrections or differential procedures are used. It is what was previously explained under GN and EKF, but with a general number of satellites.

Precise Point Positioning Precise Point Positioning (PPP) [KH07, p. 746] differs from SPP by basing the position on carrier phase measurements instead of on code range measurements. Furthermore, preciser satellite orbits and dual-frequency measurements are typically included. This can reduce the position error down to around 1 cm.

Differential GNSS   Differential GNSS [KH07, p. 709] means that fixed reference receivers transmit their positions and measurements, so that a mobile rover receiver can compute its position with more precision. This is done by correcting its pseudorange measurements, however the advantage of differential GNSS diminishes with the distance to the reference receiver(s). In some areas, active reference station networks are available, so that corrections are available also in-between reference receivers.

Real Time Kinematics   Real Time Kinematics (RTK) [KH07, p. 741] is a version of differential GNSS that also uses carrier phase measurements. It can achieve cm-level precision, and it is widely used for surveying applications.

Multi-Constellation GNSS   Multi-constellation (or multi-system) [KH07, p. 672] receivers are capable of receiving several constellations, i.e., a combination of GPS, Galileo, GLONASS, and BDS. This gives the advantage of being able to receive significantly more satellites, however multiple clock biases might have to be taken into account. Furthermore, the antenna and receiver front-end have to be adapted for multiple carrier frequencies for certain combinations.

Satellite-Based Augmentation Systems   Some countries have decided to develop their own Satellite-Based Augmentation System (SBAS) [KH07, p. 703] to make more satellites available in certain parts of the world. These satellites typically have geostationary or Tundra orbits, so that they cover the desired geographical area most of the time. Examples include Japan's Quasi-Zenith Satellite System (QZSS), India's Indian Regional Navigation Satellite System (IRNSS), USA's Wide Area Augmentation System (WAAS), and the European Geostationary Navigation Overlay Service (EGNOS) in Europe.

Accuracy of GNSS Positioning Methods   An overview of the positioning performance of different GNSS positioning methods can be found in Table 1.2, based on [KSS$^+$16]. The most difficult scenario is a moving receiver in the mountainous terrain (which is similar to an urban environment, since satellites are reflected and blocked). In this scenario, a multi-GNSS RTK receiver with QZSS is the most accurate one. More information can be found in [KH07, p. 661].

1.3   Related Work

An overview of methods to improve GNSS positioning in urban areas can be found in [BROW16]. These methods can be categorized as

1. antenna-based,

2. map-based,

3. based on fusion with external sensors and signals,

Constellations	Mode	CEP static (m)	L static	RMSE dynamic (m)	L dynamic
Open field					
Single GNSS	GPS	0.141	7.0	0.204	7.6
	DGPS	0.063	9.5	0.168	7.9
Multi-GNSS	SPP	0.217	16.0	0.767	14.0
	SPP + QZSS	0.192	16.0	0.701	14.0
	PPP	0.048	16.0	0.664	14.0
	PPP + QZSS	0.034	16.1	0.451	14.0
	RTK	0.057	18.0	0.545	15.1
	RTK + QZSS	0.031	18.7	0.152	15.6
Mountainous area					
Single GNSS	GPS	1.14	5.1	1.557	5.0
	DGPS	0.583	5.2	1.372	5.1
Multi-GNSS	SPP	2.822	10.9	8.842	15.0
	SPP + QZSS	2.694	12.0	6.384	15.1
	PPP	0.533	9.8	5.633	9.1
	PPP + QZSS	0.456	10.2	4.198	12.1
	RTK	0.717	9.6	4.871	9.9
	RTK + QZSS	0.386	10.6	1.130	10.1

Table 1.2: The table presents a comparison of the positioning accuracy for different positioning techniques, along with the number of satellites the receive on average. The values are based on [KSS+16]. DGPS is differential GPS. CEP is the circular error probable and RMSE is the root mean square error. The multi-GNSS receiver is a combination of GPS, Galileo and GLONASS. The variable L is the number of received satellites, on average.

4. received-based.

The first category [KH07, p. 612], includes placing the antenna near the ground (so that only short delays or received) or coating the reflectors with radio frequency-absorptive materials. This works in open environments in static situations, but when obstacles are present, it is beneficial to raise the antenna, so that lower elevation signals are received with less gain. A particular type of antenna is the choke ring antenna, which rejects low-elevation reflections. It can further be improved by rejecting Right Hand Circular Polarization (RHCP) signals, since the Left Hand Circular Polarization (LHCP) signals emitted by the satellites switch polarization upon reflection. Also, multiple antennas can be used, since reflections can be received differently on locations that are just around 1 m apart.

The second category includes map matching, which supports the positioning by incorporating information from geographical information systems. In many applications, this is a 2D map that can match the estimated trajectory to a road network [JSZ04]. However, 3D maps are also of interest [Gro11], since they can be combined with ray tracing to detect and mitigate reflections [LC07].

The third category is sensor fusion of GNSS with other sensors. A typical example is IMU, since it provides data that are complementary to GNSS, by outputting data that are not sensitive to the environment, at a high sampling rate. Particularly, the gyroscope of an IMU can be combined with an odometer to obtain a simple Dead Reckoning (DR) solution. This can provide a precise position in short time windows when GNSS is affected by reflections or unavailable, however drift and integration errors will quickly grow large. Other examples include sensors such as radar, lidar and camera, often in combination with approaches such as simultaneous localization and mapping [AEMR15].

The fourth category, receiver-based methods, means redesigning receiver so that they are less sensitive to reflections [KH07, p. 6 13]. From this category, one notable method that could be considered state of the art, is the multi-correlator approach [LKR08, WCL18]. By using several correlators with different delays, individual peaks (corresponding to direct signals or reflections) can be identified and compared, so that the original Line-of-Sight (LOS) peak can be used. This is, however, expensive in terms of hardware; mass-market receivers typically include few correlators. The rich information provided by the correlator output is suitable for analysis using machine learning, such as convolutional neural networks [MBC20].

This book focuses on multi-frequency methods, which are a part of the receiver-based methods (although sensor fusion-based methods are also used). Little additional hardware, low computational load, and low cost are examples of advantages of multi-frequency based methods. Multi-frequency methods have previously been used for general accuracy improvement [KRB04] or to remove the influence of Multipath (MP) on ionospheric errors [SL11, MPOC11].

Several multi-frequency methods that detect or mitigate errors caused by MP or Non-Line-of-Sight (NLOS) have already been developed, an overview is given in Table 1.3 and in [OBB18] (on which this section is based). Some systems offer three carrier frequencies, and [HLN$^+$09] discussed the advantages and disadvantages of different frequency combinations, reaching the conclusion that E1 + E5a is an optimal combination, partly since it is inter-operable with the GPS L1 and L5 bands. Triple-frequency combinations contain additional information that lowers the probability that all frequencies are identically affected by MP compared with using only two frequencies. This, however, comes at a cost of higher complexity [SG16]. The KF [Kal60], with the non-linear variants EKF and UKF are also relevant for multi-frequency signal processing. An example is to apply them on antenna arrays [LCL$^+$07], where the UKF was found to be better at estimating carrier phase MP errors than the EKF, however requiring multiple antennas.

The existing methods that detect or mitigate reflection errors can be classified in several ways, one of them is according to their input parameters. Here, three main input parameters are identified and their usage is explained: Signal-to-Noise Ratio (SNR), carrier phase, and correlator output.

SNR-Based   A first relevant input parameter is the SNR, a bandwidth-dependent quality measure of the received signal after the correlation procedure. In receivers, typically the Carrier-to-Noise-Density Ratio (C/N_0) is available, which is the SNR based on a 1 Hz bandwidth. For a given receiver-antenna configuration, the SNR is mainly influenced by the satellite elevation, decreasing for lower satellites, but also MP can influence it by constructive or destructive interference. This interference is in turn dependent on the difference in phase between direct signal and reflection, which is influenced by the carrier frequency of the signal. A review of SNR-based MP mitigation methods an be found in [LC07], where, i.e., the Modified SNR stochastic model is mentioned. This method uses dual-frequency carrier phase measurement and SNR for MP detection. Another notable method for MP detection is based on the SNR difference on multiple frequencies, for two frequencies [GJRS13], [Shi09], [vH17], [Rud12] or three frequencies [SG16]. The researchers found that a calibration based on SNR in a low MP environment can improve the results of the MP detection. These SNR difference methods are useful mainly in scenarios where the receiver movement is limited (walking speed or below [GJRS13]). SNR on several frequencies can also be used to weight the measurements differently, so that more weight is given to pseudorange measurements with less MP influence. Machine learning can be used to learn these weights, e.g., using a neural network [MCR06]. The machine learning methods, however, require large quantities of realistic and representative reflection data to train them. For lower complexity and low computational load, SNR weighting can be implemented in the receiver architecture directly, e.g., equal gain combining and adaptive gain combining, [MGCR05], [MGR05].

Carrier Phase Combination-Based   If a receiver capable of measuring the carrier phase is available (or, if a stationary reference receiver is transmitting corrections such as in RTK), carrier phase measurements can be used to compute a preciser position by providing precise pseudorange measurements. This is possible since the carrier phase measurements count the number of wavelengths that fit in the signal path between satellite and receiver. This means, however, that the so

Table 1.3: Overview of methods that can reduce positioning errors in urban areas. * = simulation, ** = real satellite acquisition; Code = code multipath error, CP = carrier phase multipath error; M = mitigation, D = detection; S = static, D = dynamic. If no information about the performance in dynamic scenarios is given, static is supposed. The table is an extended version of the one in [OBB18], ©2018 IEEE.

Method	References	Scope	Capacity	Scenario	N freq.
Unscented Kalman filter	[LCL[+]07]*	CP	M	S+D	2
Modified SNR stochastic model	[LC07]*/**	CP	D+M	S+D	2
SNR difference	[GJRS13]**, [Shi09]*/**, [vH17]**, [SG16]**	Code, CP	D	S+low-D	2, 3
SNR weighting	[MGCR05]*, [MGR05]*, [MCR06]*	MP	M	S	2
Geometry-free	[Sim06], [LZL16]*/**, [GMG[+]18]*/**, [GK88]**, [PBLO18]*/**	Code, CP	M	S+D	2, 3
Code minus carrier	[YSS11]**, [KV17]**, [PBLO18]*/**	Code	M	S	2, 3
Sideband carrier phase combination	[Shi09]*/**	Code	M	S+D	2
Modified lambda method	[SKL10]*/**	CP	M	S+D	3
Double-difference single-epoch least squares	[Lau04]*/**	CP	M	S+D	2, 3
Cocktail multiple outlier detection	[Lau05]*/**	CP	D	S+D	3
Multiple-frequency fault detection and exclusion	[LHQL17]*/**	Code	D	S	2, 3
Early late phase	[MD10a]*	CP	D	S	2
Triple-frequency linear combination	[SSR19]**	Code	M	S	3
Multipath combination	[JHS[+]19]**	Code	M	S	3, 4
Code minus phase, Multi-path linear combination	[MFG20]**	Code	M	D	2
Time differenced positioning filter	[GWS[+]20]**	Code	D	S	2
Extra-wide-lane, Narrow-lane	[GMG[+]19]**	Code	M	S	3

called integer ambiguity must be resolved, numerous methods exist for this. The carrier phase measurements are also useful for MP detection and mitigation. The work [GK88] proposed a dual-frequency method suitable for detecting stationary MP. As previously mentioned, a combination of SNR and carrier phase measurements is used in the Modified SNR stochastic model. The geometry-free linear combination is a method to cancel the geometric parts of a measurements, e.g., the ionospheric refraction [Sim06], [GMG$^+$18]. The dual-frequency version is obtained by simply computing the difference between the carrier phase and the pseudorange measurements. Ionospheric corrections can also be made in other ways, such as using a ionospheric model or by downloading corrections over a cellular network. In these situations, the dual-frequency combination is useful to mitigate MP (otherwise, a triple-frequency version is required). The double differenced geometry-free [LZL16] version is an extension that detects carrier phase MP, also working in dynamic situations. A useful method to estimate MP on two frequencies is the Code Minus Carrier (CMC) method, which combines pseudoranges based on code and carrier phase. To improve this estimation, adaptive filters have shown good results [YSS11], another possibility is to use a triple-frequency combination [KV17]. This method is of main interest for static applications, since it takes several hours for it to converge. The work [PBLO18] presents a combination of CMC and the geometry-free approach, so the numbers of excluded measurements due to MP can be reduced. This CMC-based approach can be used both for detection and for mitigation through deweighting of satellites [PBLO19]. A method to estimate carrier phase MP errors is the Sideband carrier phase combination [Shi09], which uses a carrier lock loop to estimate the error on two frequencies. This is done by analyzing the difference between the carrier phase error on both frequencies. This method's performance slightly decreases in highly dynamic situations, due to the Doppler shift getting larger between the carrier frequencies. An approach that is suitable in dynamic situations is the modified Lambda method [SKL10], where a-priori information is used in the ambiguity search process. This mitigates carrier phase MP for RTK receivers. A further method, that is applicable in both dual- and triple-frequency versions, is double-difference single-epoch least squares [CC95, Lau04]. The cocktail multiple outlier detection method [Lau05] can detect static carrier phase MP errors, but it requires reception of three carrier frequencies. Residuals on all three frequencies are tested against a threshold, however the method does not perform well when the reflectors are close, creating short reflection delays. The last method in the carrier phase category is fault detection and exclusion [HTK$^+$17], where statistical tests are used to exclude error-affected satellites. This includes MP, jamming, and also hardware errors. Extensions for dual and triple-frequency versions exist [LHQL17], which can be combined with differential positioning.

Correlator Output-Based   The correlator output can also be used to evaluate the MP situation. For multiple antennas, the analytical probability of false alarm and detection using correlator output on two frequencies has been derived [GGS11]. A notable method in the correlator output-based category is the Early late phase MP detector [MD07]. It analyzes the carrier phase difference between two correlator outputs, and the correlator spacing is a tuning parameter, with higher detection probability for larger spacing. It exists in both single- and dual-frequency versions, in the latter case it performs better, since the parameter is less likely to be near zero on both frequencies simultaneously [MD10a]. The detection threshold is C/N_0-dependent, and it depends on requirements on the probabilities of false alarm and detection. As for SNR-based methods, a reference low-multipath C/N_0-value is helpful. Since the correlator output reacts quickly to the received reflections, it is useful also for dynamic situations [PBL17].

1.4 Contributions and Outline of this book

The pseudorange measurement errors caused by MP, NLOS, and blocked satellites in urban areas are non-Gaussian and they change quickly. This has a heavy impact when positioning algorithms such as EKF or Gauss-Newton are used, since small errors centered around zero are assumed. This book addresses this issue, first by characterizing the measurement urban errors in urban canyons. This is done for signals on two carrier frequencies, the GPS L1 and the GPS L2 signal. Thereafter, the problem is treated using novel multi-frequency signal processing methods. This starts with classifying the reception mode of each satellite using dual-frequency observables (such as pseudorange as SNR). Subsequently, the satellites that are received MP are specifically analyzed, so that their MP can be estimated and their pseudorange measurements corrected. This is a type of MP mitigation, since the satellites are not excluded, but their measurements are corrected. Finally, positioning in an urban canyon is studied, where realistic measurement are simulated in an urban scenario, so that the resulting positioning accuracy can be analyzed and compared. The common theme for all chapters of this book is thus multi-frequency GNSS, with the red thread going from characterization, to detection, via mitigation, and finally accurate positioning. In Fig. 1.8, the relation between the chapters can be studied, they support each other in different ways.

Characterization of Reflections in Urban C anyons – Chapter 2 . To get a better understanding of the positioning errors of GNSS in urban canyons, a simulation that includes a 3D urban environment is presented. In this environment, a vehicle is moving, and for each time step, ray tracing is used to determine which signals that are reflected or blocked on their from satellite to the receiver. The chapter offers four contributions. The first one is to give the distributions of the underlying reflection parameters: reflection delay, Reflection Ratio (RR), reflection Doppler difference, and reflection phase shift. This is done grouped by the simulated building height and by the satellite elevation, which is an easily accessible parameter in most receivers. The second contribution is a method to estimate the reflection delay distribution using the number of received satellites, which supports MP delay estimation methods such as the one presented in Chapter 4. The third contribution is an analysis of the distribution of the pseudorange errors in urban canyons, on two carrier frequencies. This is important when an algorithm is using these measurements to estimate the receiver position, which is done in Chapter 5. Fourth, the simulation code itself is a contribution; researchers can download the code to create their own geometric configuration and

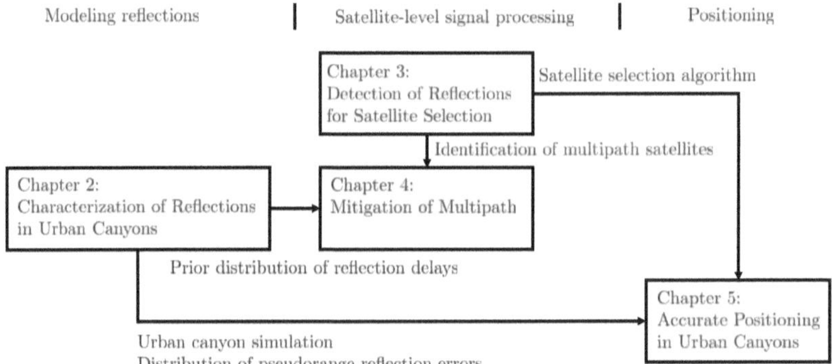

Figure 1.8: The chapters of this book are related according to this flow chart.

positioning algorithm, giving quick and comparable results.

Detection of Reflections for Satellite S election – Chapter 3 . In urban canyons of moderate building height, where enough error-free satellites are still available, the satellites affected by NLOS or MP can be detected and their measurements excluded from the positioning algorithm. Two contributions are made in this area. First, two algorithms to classify the reception mode of a satellite, based on its dual-frequency correlator output are presented. These satellite classification algorithms can be used for satellite selection, or to identify MP satellites whose pseudorange can be corrected according to Chapter 4. Second, an algorithm to select the satellites with the smallest pseudorange errors is presented, using SNR and pseudoranges as input, also on two carrier frequencies. This is then used for satellite selection in Chapter 5, since the positioning algorithm is sensitive to pseudorange measurements that quickly change due to reflections.

Mitigation of Multipath – Chapter 4. Satellites that are received as MP still have contact with the receiver through the direct signal, making it possible to correct the pseudorange errors if the reflection delay is known. The contribution is a method to estimate this reflection delay, based on signal power measurements on multiple carrier frequencies. The measurement noise on signal power measurements is analyzed through a hardware experiment, and a corresponding Maximum Likelihood (ML) estimation problem is derived and solved. This is especially helpful in urban areas with tight streets and tall buildings, where every available satellite is important for accurate positioning.

Accurate Positioning in Urban Canyons – Chapter 5. The last contribution takes the urban canyon navigation problem into the positioning domain, by exploiting the pseudorange measurements on multiple frequencies to estimate the position of several receivers. The previously mentioned satellite selection algorithm is used to exclude MP and NLOS satellites, while fusion with data from Vehicle to Vehicle Communication (V2V) and DR is performed. The contribution is a method to combine these measurements with an EKF, together with a comparison that shows how much each data source helps to reduce the positioning error. It can be seen as a platform, capable of including whichever measurements that are available (between dual-frequency GNSS, V2V, and DR) to compute the most accurate positioning that it can, given the available data.

Chapter 2

Characterization of Reflections in Urban Canyons

In this chapter, we start by characterizing the errors caused by reflections on GNSS receivers in urban areas. Twelve urban areas with different building heights are generated, and the signals that reach a moving receiver are analyzed. In this way, a basic understanding of the nature of GNSS reception in urban canyons is achieved. How large the pseudorange errors typically are, and which distribution they follow is studied. This is important, since filters for position estimation (such as the EKF, discussed in Section 5.4) make certain assumptions about the statistical distribution of the measurement errors.

> This chapter is primarily based on [OBB20b], with the addition of the distributions of RR, Doppler shift difference, phase shift, and pseudorange errors.

First, the problem is formulated in Section 2.1 and Section 2.2 presents related work. Second, a 3D urban area simulation is detailed in Section 2.3, while Section 2.4 explains how ray tracing is applied to generate reflections. Third, Section 2.5 presents the distribution of the reception modes. Fourth, the resulting distributions of reflection delays are given in Section 2.6, along with a method to estimate these distributions based on the number of satellites. Thereafter, the distributions of RR (Section 2.7), the Doppler shift difference (Section 2.8), and the pseudorange errors (Section 2.9) are presented. Finally, Section 2.10 gives a brief discussion, while Section 2.11 concludes this chapter.

2.1 Problem Formulation

In order to determine the position of a receiver, pseudorange measurements from L satellites, indexed by l

$$\rho^l = \sqrt{(r^x - s^{l,x})^2 + (r^y - s^{l,y})^2 + (r^z - s^{l,z})^2} + b + w^l + v_\rho \tag{2.1}$$

are central, where b is the receiver clock bias in meters, w^l is the error caused by reflections and v_ρ is Gaussian measurement noise with zero mean and standard deviation σ_ρ.

The variables $s^{l,x}$, $s^{l,y}$, and $s^{l,z}$ represent the ECEF position of the satellite l. Each satellite sends data on two carrier frequencies, thus a second pseudorange is obtained

$$\underline{\rho}^l = \sqrt{(r^x - s^{l,x})^2 + (r^y - s^{l,y})^2 + (r^z - s^{l,z})^2} + b + \underline{w}^l + \underline{v}_\rho, \tag{2.2}$$

where $\underline{w}^l$ is the error caused by reflections, and $\underline{v}_\rho$ is Gaussian measurement noise with zero mean and standard deviation $\underline{\sigma}_\rho$.

The distributions of the reflection pseudorange errors on each frequency w^l and $\underline{w}^l$ will depend on the geometrical configuration of the urban area. The goal of this chapter is to study these distributions. The pseudorange error also depends on which tracking method that the receiver uses, as well as on four underlying reflection parameters: the reception mode, the reflection delay, the reflection power loss and the reflection Doppler difference. For this reason, the distributions of these four parameters are also given, so that receiver-independent results can be presented.

2.2   Related Work

Reflection distributions in urban canyons can be analyzed in two ways: by simulation or by directly measuring satellites. In the following paragraphs, related work is discussed grouped by these two categories.

Measuring Reflections   To measure reflection distributions, a receiver capable of measuring reflections is required [SA03, XP15, UCPY12, MGZC18]. This receiver can then be mounted be on a car roof and transported around in urban area, recording all reflections that are encountered. This leads to realistic results that are representative of the urban area that was used. On the other hand, the results might not be valid for other urban areas and accurate hardware is needed so that the reflections are accurately recorded. By measuring reflections in Shanghai, [WCL18] found that the reflection delays follow a gamma distribution [HC78, p. 103], whose shape parameter is related to the number of times each signal is reflected on average. The reflections were measured using a receiver equipped with multiple correlators, making it possible to distinguish individual reflections from each other and the direct signal. The work [XP15] measured reflections in downtown Calgary in Canada, and analyzed the resulting correlator output and the Doppler shifts. It concludes that a high C/N_0 is required to separate the direct signal from reflections, and that this becomes easier at higher speeds. Furthermore, it concludes that the correlator peaks of the direct signal and the reflection are often hard to distinguish, depending on the used correlator map.

Simulating Reflections   The second way is to simulate MP distributions, by generating a 3D environment and implementing ray tracing to identify the reflections [SL04, LS05, SLS09, Ger19,

ERKH04]. Noteworthy is the work of the German Aerospace Center [SA03, SL04], which measured GNSS-like signals emitted from a zeppelin, and then developed a more general MATLAB simulation based on those data. In [ERKH04], a 3D environment combined with ray tracing was used similarly to the method in this chapter, but in order to evaluate adaptive antenna algorithms in MP environments. A 3D environment can also be generated by software, to recreate reflected signals in a hardware GNSS generator [Spi20]. An advantage of simulations is that the environment can be easily varied (from relatively open suburban areas to dense urban canyons), and the method is quite simple if the signals are limited to only reflecting once. However, the complexity of multi-reflection simulations grow exponentially as more reflectors are present. Furthermore, a validation with real data is usually necessary with algorithms based on simulations.

To summarize, related work can both be based on measurement in real environment and on simulations (in both software and hardware). There is however a lack of openly available and flexible simulation software.

2.3 Urban Canyon Model

A MATLAB simulation was setup to generate a 3D urban area with nine city blocks, where the buildings are 25 m wide and their height is a random variable that follows a Rice distribution [Ric45]

$$h \sim \text{Rice}(\nu, 5\,\text{m}). \tag{2.3}$$

The non-deterministic height gives the simulated urban area more realism. In a real city, all buildings rarely have the same height, and satellites can quickly disappear and reappear when the receiver suddenly passes nearby a taller building. The Rice distribution was chosen because a strictly positive distribution is required (all buildings must be taller than 0 m). The variable ν is the non-centrality parameter, which will increase the average building height. A spread of 5 m was used for all simulations, so that the building heights vary in a way similar to a real urban canyon (this was based on satellite photos and 3D maps of Manhattan in the center of New York City). The side of each square city block is 250 m and a road of width 30 m separates them, Fig. 2.1. Since the receiver only moves in the inner area of the simulated city, all buildings along the outer side were removed, creating a cross shape. This was done to decrease the computational load of the ray tracing, Section 2.4. The Rice distribution only supports positive values, and its mean (for the spread of 5 m) is

$$\mu = 5\sqrt{\frac{\pi}{2}} L_{1/2}\left(\frac{-\nu^2}{50}\right), \tag{2.4}$$

where $L_{1/2}$ is the Laguerre polynomial of degree $1/2$. This mean is slightly above the non-centrality parameter, mainly for low building heights. Thus, the non-centrality parameter ν can be interpreted as a variable that is close to the mean building height of the urban area.

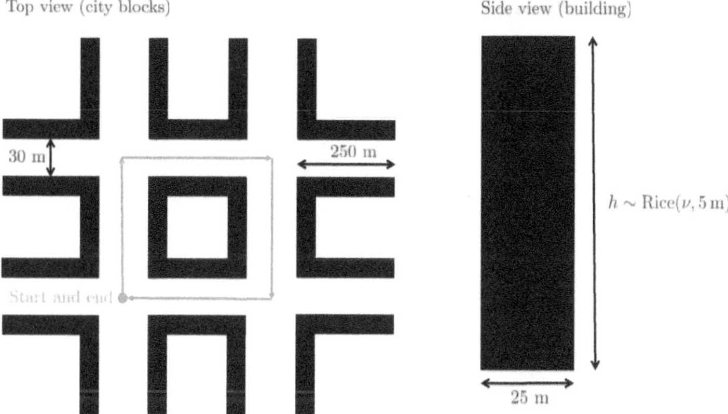

Figure 2.1: On the left, the top view of the urban area is seen, following deterministic road and block widths. To the right, a single building is visualized from the side, it has a deterministic width, but the height follows a Rice distribution. The figure is adapted from [OBB18].

Environments To generate results from urban areas with varying building heights, 12 environments were generated, each with different values of ν, that varied from 5 m to 60 m in steps of 5 m, see Fig. 2.2. In this way, results from an area with low buildings $\nu = 5\,\text{m}$ representing a suburban area can be seen, and compared with urban canyons, where $\nu = 60\,\text{m}$. As an example, Fig. 2.3 shows a generated urban environment, where $\nu = 25\,\text{m}$ can be seen.

Vehicle A cuboid with identical sides of 2 m, and a height of 1.5 m represents the vehicle. It has an antenna placed on the center on its roof, with a distance above the roof of 1 cm. The vehicle velocity is $\dot{\mathbf{r}}$ and its speed is $\|\dot{\mathbf{r}}\| = 5$ m/s. The vehicle drives a full turn around the central city block, driving in the middle of the road, see Fig. 2.1. The vehicle drives a distance of 1.12 km, which represents 224 s of time in the simulation. The scenario is sampled at 2 Hz.

Satellites The number of received satellites and their maximal elevation depend on the latitude, which is why an intermediate latitude was chosen near New York City: $\phi = 40°, \lambda = -70°$. The positions of all 31 GPS satellites were generated using a modified version of the software of [S. 18]. The simulation of each environment was repeated six times, fast-forwarding the satellite constellation two hours each repetition. The purpose of this to obtain constellation-independent results. As seen from the receiver, the elevation of a satellite is θ and its azimuth angle is β, see Fig. 2.4. At these selected coordinates, around eight satellites are above 15° elevation on average, which is what a typical receiver would use in a completely open environment. The simulation was

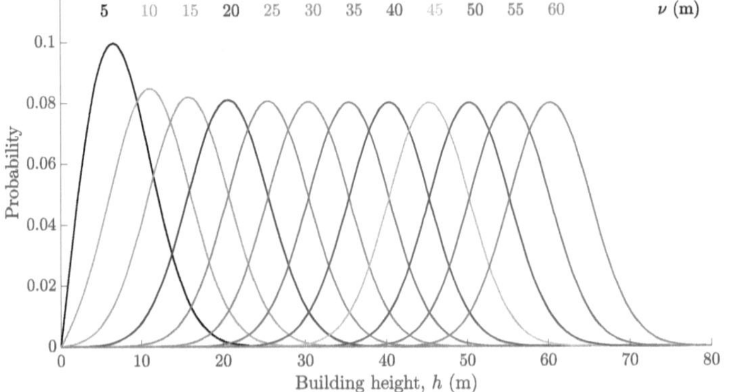

Figure 2.2: 12 environments were simulated, each with a different mean building height (represented by a different Rician non-centrality parameter). The figure is adapted from [OBB18].

done based on the two main carrier frequencies of GPS and Galileo $f_1 = 1.5754\,\text{GHz}$ (GPS L1 and Galileo E1) and $f_2 = 1.2276\,\text{GHz}$ (GPS L2 and Galileo E5b).

2.4   Ray Tracing of Reflections

Next, given the positions of all satellites and the position of the receiver, the possible paths between them (direct or reflected) have to be identified. This is done with ray tracing, and for this, each building is represented by five planes: all the walls and the roof. The ground is represented by a single large plane. All these planes are stored in a large list, so it can be checked which signals they reflected, which they block, and which signals they do not influence. The implemented version of ray tracing only checks for first-level reflections, i.e., a specific path from a satellite to the receiver can be reflected once at the most. For this, the satellite position s, the receiver position r and all the planes generated in Section 2.3 are required. Each plane is defined by a point on it q_{point}, its normal q_{normal} and its limits.

The following process is repeated for each time step, plane, and satellite. First, the receiver position is mirrored in the plane, see Fig. 2.4

$$q_{\text{mirr}} = r + 2q_{\text{normal}} \left(\frac{(q_{\text{point}} - r) \cdot q_{\text{normal}}}{q_{\text{normal}} \cdot q_{\text{normal}}} \right). \tag{2.5}$$

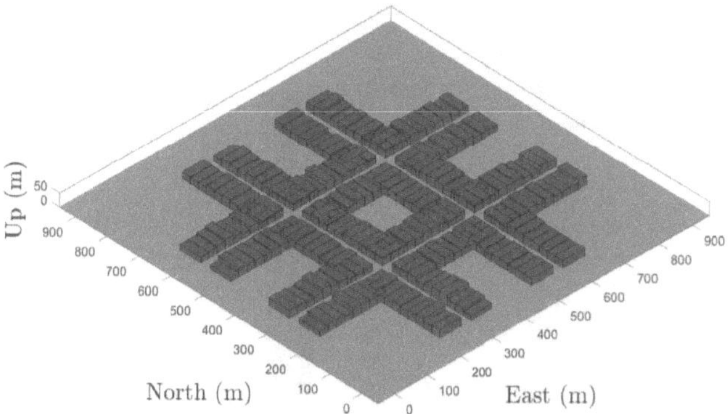

Figure 2.3: A generated urban area, where the height of all buildings follow a Rice distribution with $\nu = 25\,\mathrm{m}$. The figure is adapted from [OBB18].

Second, projection is used to identify the reflection point in the plane

$$\mathbf{q}_{\mathrm{refl}} = \mathbf{s} + \frac{(\mathbf{q}_{\mathrm{point}} - \mathbf{s}) \cdot \mathbf{q}_{\mathrm{normal}}}{(\mathbf{q}_{\mathrm{mirr}} - \mathbf{s}) \cdot \mathbf{q}_{\mathrm{normal}}} (\mathbf{q}_{\mathrm{mirr}} - \mathbf{s}). \qquad (2.6)$$

Third, a test whether $\mathbf{q}_{\mathrm{refl}}$ is within the limits of the plane is made; the reflection is only saved if this is true. The process from (2.5) to (2.6) is repeated for all planes in the scenario (the four walls and the roof of each building, and the ground). For the subsequent analysis, only reflections on buildings are taken into account. A large number of the reflections reflect on the car roof, where $d < 1\,\mathrm{cm}$ (the distance of the antenna above the car roof), but these are ignored. Ground reflections could also theoretically occur, but none were found in the simulation, since they were also blocked by the car body.

2.5 Distribution of Reception Modes

To start with, it is relevant to see how the satellites are received in each urban environment, i.e., the reception modes. Four reception modes are possible: Single Path Line-of-Sight (SPLOS) means receiving only the direct signal, MP is a direct signal and at least one reflection, NLOS means receiving only reflections, and a satellite can also be completely blocked, see Fig. 2.5. If four or more satellites are received as SPLOS, a satellite selection can be done (as in Chapter 3), so that an accurate position can be computed using a subset of satellites with low pseudorange measurement errors. Otherwise, MP reception results in interference than can create a widely

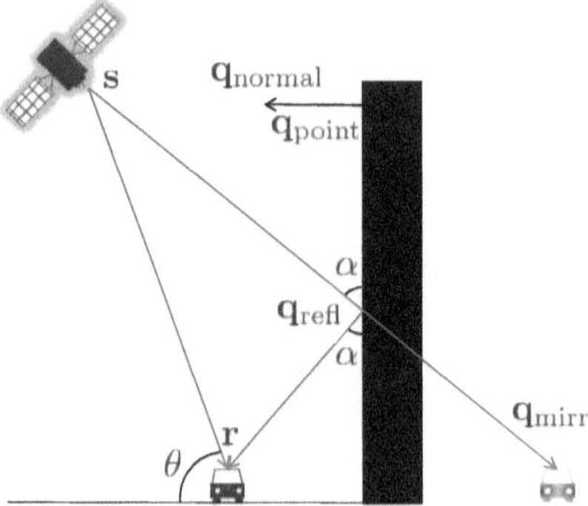

Figure 2.4: To generate a reflection, the receiver with position $\mathbf{r}$ is mirrored in the building plane. The figure is adapted from [OBB20b].

varying pseudorange error, while NLOS typically causes the receiver to erroneously track the reflection. This is why the reception mode is of interest.

As the buildings of the urban canyon increase in height, fewer satellites are received as SPLOS and more are blocked, see Fig. 2.6. Furthermore, with increasing urban canyon depth, the MP becomes slightly less common, while the opposite is true for NLOS. This can be explained since the taller buildings block more direct signals and they also block more reflections (as can be seen in Fig. 2.7). By summing the number of satellites in the reception modes SPLOS, MP and NLOS, the total number of received satellites L is obtained. The critical point $L < 4$ is reached somewhere between $\nu = 40\,\mathrm{m}$ and $\nu = 45\,\mathrm{m}$. After this, 3D positioning using only GNSS is not feasible and sensor fusion with, e.g., IMU becomes necessary.

2.6 Distribution of Reflection Delays

By computing the path difference between the direct signal and the signal that is taking the path via the reflection point, the reflection delay

$$d = \|\mathbf{q}_{\mathrm{refl}} - \mathbf{s}\| + \|\mathbf{r} - \mathbf{q}_{\mathrm{refl}}\| - \|\mathbf{r} - \mathbf{s}\| \tag{2.7}$$

is obtained, see Fig. 2.8. GNSS receivers work by measuring time-of-flight, resulting in a delay measured in seconds. However, in this work, to make it easier to relate the delay to the geometrical configuration in the urban canyon, it is transformed to meters by multiplying with the speed of

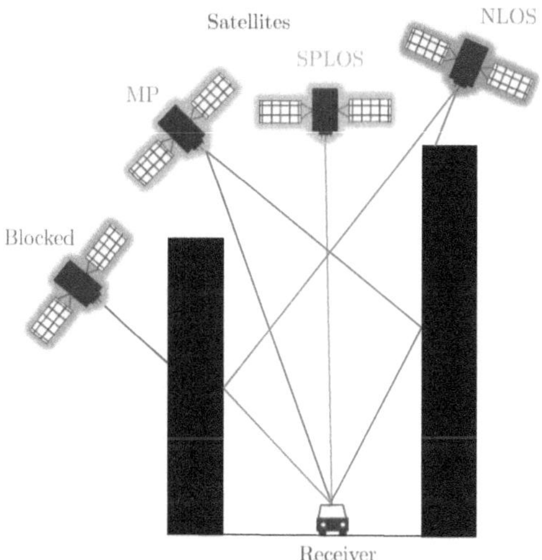

Figure 2.5: A satellite can be received according to four modes: only a direct signal is Single Path Line-of-Sight (SPLOS), a direct signal and at least one reflection is Multipath (MP), only reflections is Non-Line-of-Sight (NLOS), or blocked. The figure is adapted from [OBB18], ©2018 IEEE.

light in vacuum c. Note however, that the atmosphere is not a vacuum, thus the speed of light is slightly differs there in reality, but this is compensated in the receiver as atmospheric effects.

Fig. 2.9 presents the distribution of d as a function of the building height parameter ν. We can see that the delays are concentrated at rather small values (around 15 m), with a few delays reaching large values of up to 800 m. The reflections get smaller as the urban canyon height increases. A reasonable explanation is that the longer reflections tend to get blocked more when the buildings are taller, making these reflections rare in deep urban canyons. If, however, taller buildings are present further away, these longer reflections could become more common.

The distribution of d for different elevation angles θ can be found in Fig. 2.10. Most reflections delays are smaller than 30 m, and in general, satellites with higher elevation angles produce reflections with smaller delays, except for the first elevation bin of $0° < \theta \leq 15°$. Again, a few outlier reflections have a delay of up to 800 m.

Estimating Reflection Delay Distributions Using the Number of Satellites   The focus of Chapter 4 is to estimate the MP delay as a way of identifying the pseudorange error. For this purpose, a prior distribution on the delay d is of interest. By plotting the Probability Density Function (PDF)

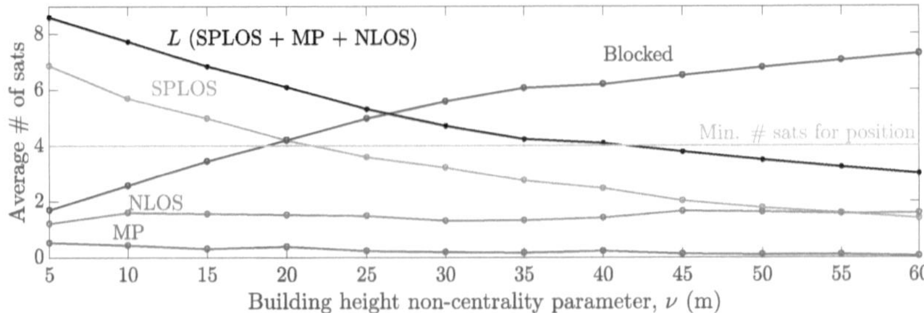

Figure 2.6: The average number of satellites in each of the four reception modes depends on how tall the buildings are. The figure is adapted from [OBB20b].

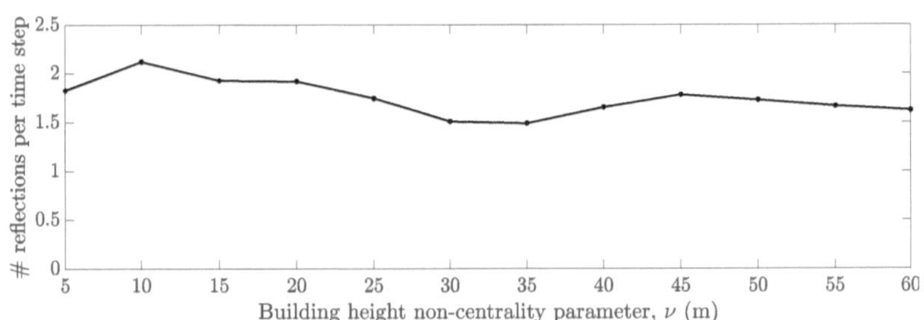

Figure 2.7: On average, around two reflections are received per time step (mean across all six constellation repetitions), but fewer reflections are received where the buildings are tall. The figure is adapted from [OBB20b].

of the reflection delays (making the area of the bars to sum to 1), as opposed to the normalization method used Fig. 2.9, where the bar heights sum to 1, we can see that a gamma distribution with a shape parameter that is the median reflection delay quite well approximates most reflection delays, see Fig. 2.11. The scale parameter is set to 1, regardless of the building heights. The few delays that are very large (more than 80 m) are however ignored, so that a Probability Density Function (PDF) that reasonably approximates the most delays can be found. These large delays are also the reason for using the median as shape parameter, instead of, e.g., the mean. The receiver can easily compute the number of satellites L that are reaching it. As seen in Fig. 2.6, the number of satellites decreases as the building height increases, as is the case with the median reflection delay. Thus, using the least-squares algorithm, a simple model can be achieved, that allows estimation of

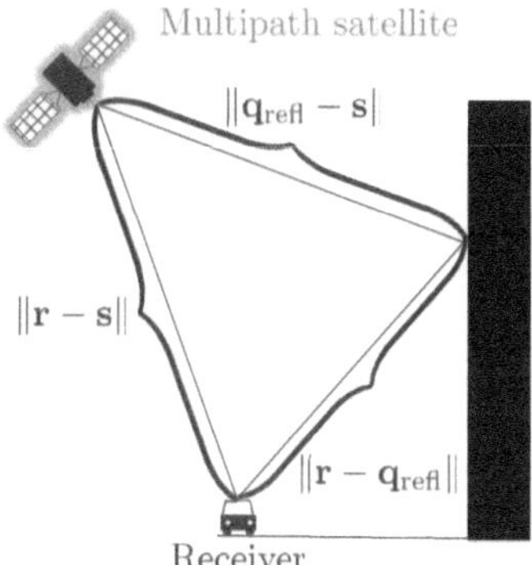

Figure 2.8: The reflection has a delay with respect to the direct path. The figure is adapted from [OBB20a].

the median delay based on the number of satellites, see Fig. 2.12

$$\hat{d}_m = -0.23L^2 + 5.08L - 4.08. \tag{2.8}$$

Note that (2.8) is simply a data-based parameter of a second-degree polynomial to the results of the simulation, based only on GPS. A parameter adaption is necessary for it to generalize to other or multiple constellations. Furthermore, each polynomial coefficient needs a correct conversion factor to end up with a median delay with a unit of meters.

The Root Mean Square (RMS) estimation error of the median delay for the model is

$$\sqrt{\frac{1}{N}\sum_{n=1}^{N}(\hat{d}_{m,n} - d_{m,n})^2} = 0.33\,\mathrm{m}. \tag{2.9}$$

This model is only suitable for receivers that are working only with GPS. For a multi-constellation receiver (that receives, e.g., Galileo as well), one must adjust the coefficients in 2.8. An overview of the process to use the number of received satellites to get a prior distribution on the reflection delay is presented in Fig. 2.13. A patent for this procedure is pending [OB20b].

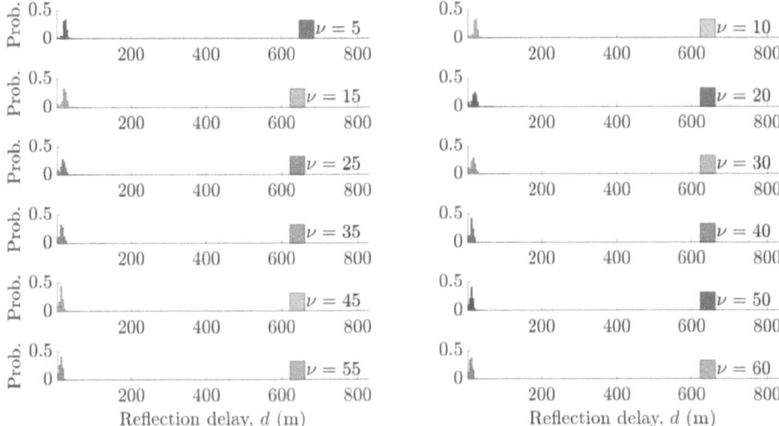

Figure 2.9: Higher urban areas tend to concentrate the reflection delays around smaller values. A few outliers values are above 80 m, for a zoomed-in version, see Fig. 2.11.

2.7 Distribution of Reflection Ratio and Phase Shift

The pseudorange does not only depend on the reflection delay, the RR and the phase shift of the reflection also play an important role. To compute these two parameters, the complex reflection coefficient Γ is of use [Flo87, p. 246], [Han01]. The complex reflection coefficient in turn, depends on the material of the reflection point $\mathbf{q}_{\text{refl}}$, specifically the relative permittivity κ_r and the electrical conductivity γ. Based on these two variables, the complex dielectric constant

$$\kappa = \kappa_r - j\frac{60c\gamma}{f} \tag{2.10}$$

can be formed, which depends on the carrier frequency f. In the simulations, all buildings consist of concrete, with $\kappa_r = 3$ and $\gamma = 200\,\text{mS/m}$.

The effective reflection coefficient

$$\Gamma_e = \left(|\Gamma_c| + 10^{\frac{-\eta\sin(\theta)}{20\,\text{dB}}}|\Gamma_x|\right)e^{-j\pi} \tag{2.11}$$

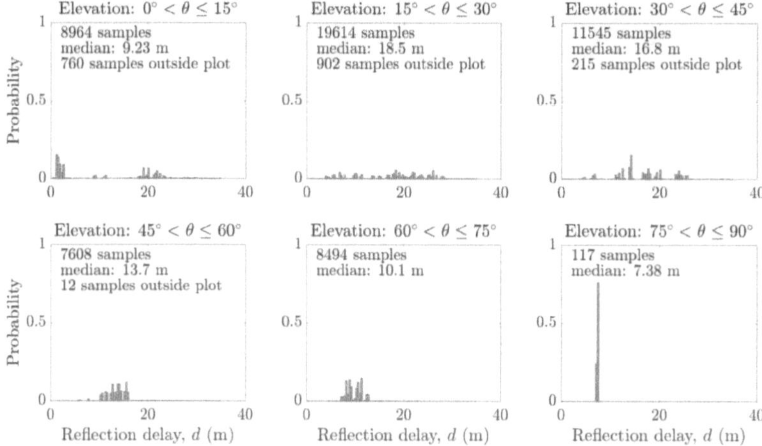

Figure 2.10: Higher elevation satellites tend to concentrate the reflection delays around smaller values.

consists of two components, a co-polar

$$\Gamma_c = \frac{\Gamma_h + \Gamma_v}{2} \tag{2.12}$$

and a cross-polar one

$$\Gamma_x = \frac{\Gamma_h - \Gamma_v}{2}, \tag{2.13}$$

which in turn can be expressed as a function of effective reflection coefficient κ in their horizontal

$$\Gamma_h = \frac{\sin(\alpha) - \sqrt{\kappa - \cos^2(\alpha)}}{\sin(\alpha) + \sqrt{\kappa - \cos^2(\alpha)}}, \tag{2.14}$$

and vertical

$$\Gamma_v = \frac{\kappa \sin(\alpha) - \sqrt{\kappa - \cos^2(\alpha)}}{\kappa \sin(\alpha) + \sqrt{\kappa - \cos^2(\alpha)}} \tag{2.15}$$

components. The reflection angle α is visualized in Fig. 2.4, while $\eta = 3\,\mathrm{dB}$ is the LHCP rejection ratio of the antenna.

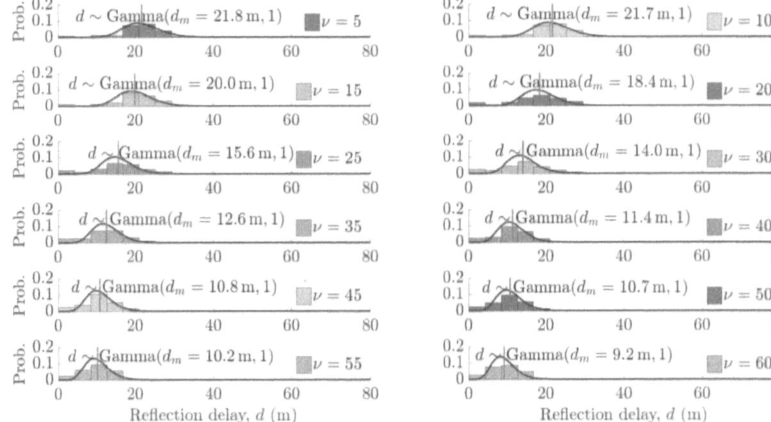

Figure 2.11: Urban areas with different building heights result in different reflection delay distributions. These distributions can be approximated by a gamma distribution, with the median reflection delay as shape parameter. The figure is adapted from [OBB20b].

To obtain the RR, the absolute value of the effective reflection coefficient is computed

$$\Lambda = |\Gamma_e|,\tag{2.16}$$

while the phase shift is the argument

$$\Phi = \arg(\Gamma_e).\tag{2.17}$$

The distribution of the RR as a function of the building height can be found in Fig. 2.14. The urban areas with lower building height result in weaker reflections, with values of $\Lambda \approx 0.4$. For urban areas with higher buildings ($\nu > 55\,\mathrm{m}$), we see the values of the RR concentrating around 0.6. The reflections are weaker at lower elevation angles, while for higher elevation satellites, most reflections have an RR slightly higher than 0.5, meaning that reflections are just above half the strength of the direct signal, see Fig. 2.15. The simulation resulted in a phase shift of $\Phi = \pi\,\mathrm{rad}$ for all reflections, regardless of the building height parameter or satellite elevation.

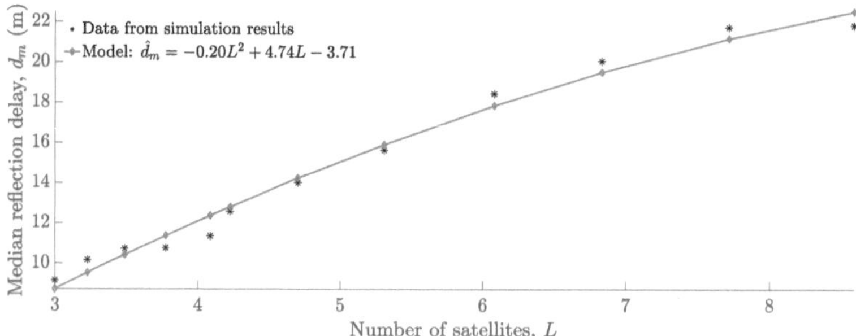

Figure 2.12: A second-degree polynomial can predict the median reflection delay based on the number of received satellites. The number of satellites L is an average across several repated simulations, thus the data points are non-integer values. The figure is adapted from [OBB20b].

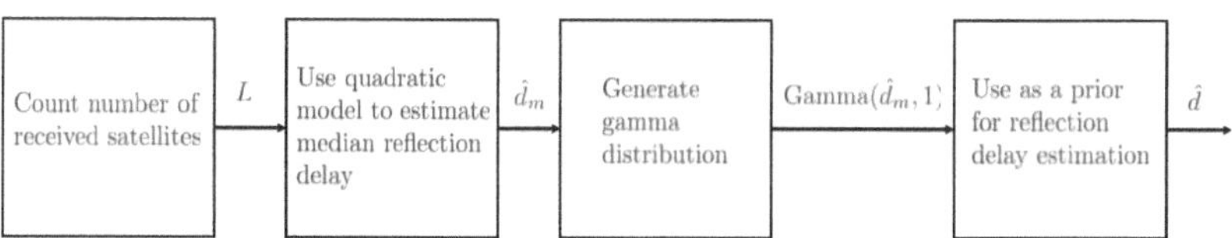

Figure 2.13: The gamma distribution of the reflection delays is useful for reflection delay estimation problems. The figure is adapted from [OBB20b].

2.8 Distribution of Reflection Doppler Difference

The Doppler shift of the direct signal will not be identical to the Doppler shift of the reflection, since these two signals typically arrive at the receiver from different directions. The Doppler shift of the direct signal is

$$f_{\mathrm{D}}^{\mathrm{LOS}} = f \frac{c\|\mathbf{s} - \mathbf{r}\| - \left(\dot{\mathbf{r}} \cdot (\mathbf{s} - \mathbf{r})\right)}{c\|\mathbf{s} - \mathbf{r}\| - \left(\dot{\mathbf{s}} \cdot (\mathbf{s} - \mathbf{r})\right)}, \tag{2.18}$$

where c is the speed of light in vacuum, f is the emitted carrier frequency by the satellite, $\mathbf{s}$ and $\mathbf{r}$ are the satellite and receiver positions, respectively. The variables $\dot{\mathbf{s}}$ and $\dot{\mathbf{r}}$ are the velocities of the satellite and the receiver, respectively.

Similarly, the Doppler shift at the reflection point is

$$f_{\mathrm{D}}^{\mathbf{q}_{\mathrm{refl}}} = f \frac{c\|\mathbf{s} - \mathbf{q}_{\mathrm{refl}}\|}{c\|\mathbf{s} - \mathbf{q}_{\mathrm{refl}}\| - \left(\dot{\mathbf{s}} \cdot (\mathbf{s} - \mathbf{q}_{\mathrm{refl}})\right)}. \tag{2.19}$$

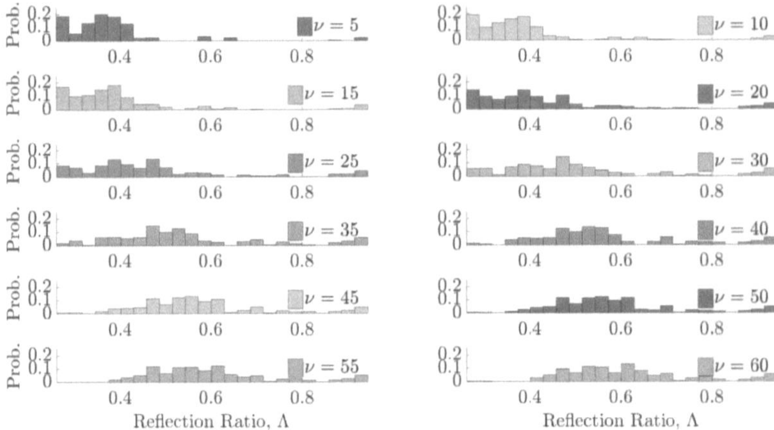

Figure 2.14: Deeper urban areas typically result in stronger reflections.

The Doppler shift of the reflection at the receiver is then

$$f_D^{\text{refl}} = f_D^{\mathbf{q}_{\text{refl}}} \frac{c\|\mathbf{q}_{\text{refl}} - \mathbf{r}\| - \left(\dot{\mathbf{r}} \cdot (\mathbf{q}_{\text{refl}} - \mathbf{r})\right)}{c\|\mathbf{q}_{\text{refl}} - \mathbf{r}\|}. \tag{2.20}$$

Finally, the Doppler shift difference between direct signal and reflection is

$$\Upsilon = f_D^{\text{refl}} - f_D^{\text{LOS}}. \tag{2.21}$$

The Doppler shift difference is highly concentrated at small values around 1 Hz, with a few outliers at $\pm 50\,\text{Hz}$, see Fig. 2.16 and Fig. 2.17. The elevation angle or the urban canyon building height of the satellite do not change the distribution significantly. The smaller values are due to it being a Doppler shift difference between direct signal, and not a Doppler shift by itself. A zoomed-in version of Fig. 2.16 can be found in Fig. 2.18. The zoomed-in values near 0 Hz follow a similar pattern for all building heights. In Fig. 2.19, the probabiltiy axis is logarithmic, for better appreciation of the smaller Doppler shift differences.

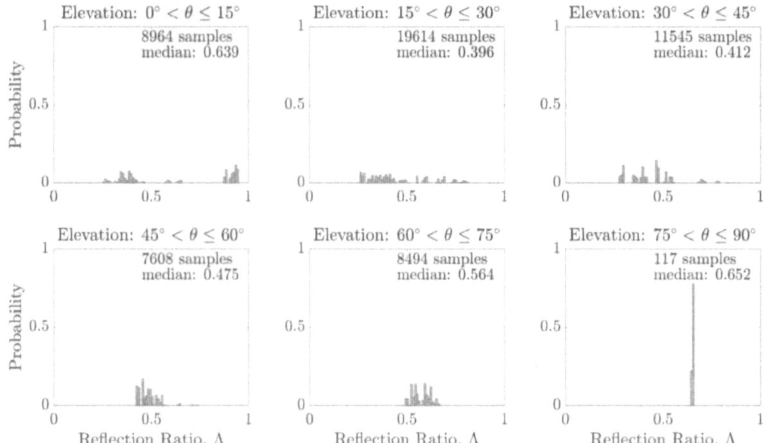

Figure 2.15: The strength of the reflections tends to be slightly over half the strength of the direct signals at higher elevations, while for lower elevations the strength is spread out on a larger interval.

2.9 Distribution of Pseudorange Errors

Now, the physical characteristics and their distributions have been explained. However, depending on the tracking method used by the receiver, these reflection characteristics will result in different pseudorange errors w and $\underline{w}$. First, the LOS signal (if present) and all reflections are summed. We make the assumption that maximally one reflection is present. This is not always the case in real situations, but typically one of the reflections is significantly stronger than others [KH07, p. 602]. Thus, we have the direct signal

$$g_{\text{LOS}}(t) = \sqrt{2P_{\text{LOS}}} \cos\left(2\pi(f + f_{\text{D}}^{\text{LOS}})t\right) + v_g, \tag{2.22}$$

and a reflection

$$g_{\text{refl}}(t) = \sqrt{2P_{\text{LOS}}} = \Lambda \cos\left(2\pi(f + f_{\text{D}}^{\text{refl}})(t + \frac{d}{c}) + \Phi\right) + v_g, \tag{2.23}$$

where P_{LOS} is the power of the direct signal and v_g is Gaussian measurement noise with zero mean and standard deviation σ_g. Due to the CDMA channel method (that allows the satellites to be distinguished), the receiver cannot access the direct signal and the reflection separately, but it will

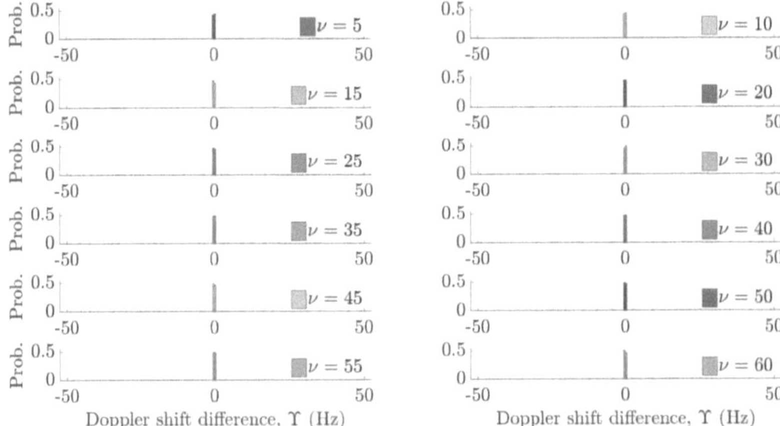

Figure 2.16: For all urban canyon height values, the Doppler shift between direct signals and reflections is typically small, around 1 Hz.

receiver them as a sum

$$g(t) = g_{\text{LOS}}(t) + g_{\text{refl}}(t) = \sqrt{2P_{\text{LOS}}}\left(\cos\left(2\pi(f + f_D^{\text{LOS}})t\right) + \Lambda\cos\left(2\pi(f + f_D^{\text{refl}})(t + \frac{d}{c}) + \Phi\right) \right) + v_g.$$

$$(2.24)$$

Even if a receiver capable of directly sampling $g(t)$ was available (this would require a sampling rate of around 3 GHz), it would thus receive a mix of signals from different satellites, possibly with reflections included. For these reasons, it is more meaningful to work with the output that comes from the tracking procedure. The tracking method is mainly decided by the correlator, there are correlators that are specifically designed to reduce MP errors [vDFF92, GvDJM96]. The correlator is typically a non-linear function and it computes the pseudorange based on the summed signal, see Fig. 2.20

$$\hat{\rho} = \text{Correlator}\big(g(t)\big).$$

$$(2.25)$$

This means that small variations in the reflection characteristics can result in widely different pseudorange errors, depending on, e.g., the interference of the two signals. A receiver using three correlator points, spaced 0.5 chips apart was simulated to compute pseudoranges based on the

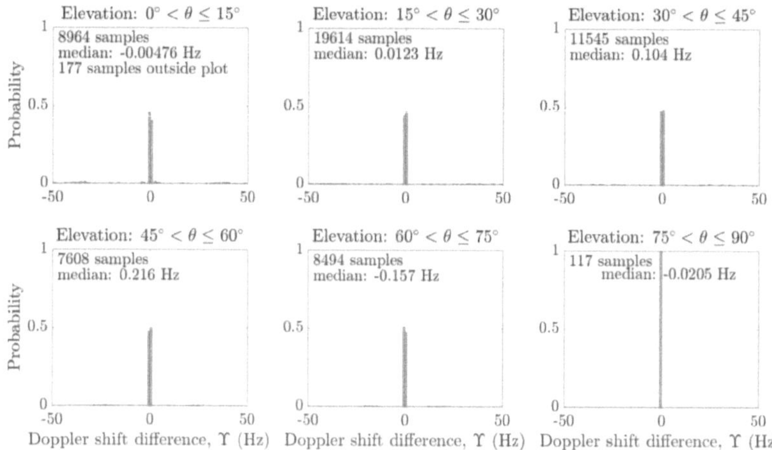

Figure 2.17: For all elevation angles, the Doppler shift between direct signals and reflections is typically small, around 1 Hz.

reflection parameters. The correlator determines the pseudorange by finding a point where the early and late correlator points have approximately equal power, and where the phase correlator power is high. Fig. 2.21 illustrates the correlator under MP reception ($d = 101.5\,$m and $\Lambda = 3.56$). The pseudorange error varies widely across the two signals, since their different carrier frequencies causes different interference.

All received signals of the simulation with $\nu = 30\,$m (regardless of reception mode) were fed into the receiver simulation, resulting in the pseudorange error distribution of Fig. 2.22 (GPS L1 signal) and Fig. 2.23 (GPS L2 signal). First, it is interesting to note that the type of signal and carrier frequency seem to influence the pseudorange error distribution only marginally. Second, we can identify the main reason why reflection errors are a difficult problem: their distribution is non-Gaussian, with a majority being near zero. However, around 13 m, the probability gets again higher. Furthermore, a few errors are around the maximum values near $\pm\,300$ m. The large concentration of errors around 0 m represent satellites that are received mainly through SPLOS, while the concentration at around 13 m is mainly MP errors. These have a tendency to be positive, the reflection delay is always positive. The negative pseudorange errors are mostly caused by destructive interference, that heavily corrupts the correlation form. The very large positive outliers are mainly caused by NLOS. Zoomed-in versions of Fig. 2.22 and Fig. 2.23 can be found in Fig. 2.24 and Fig. 2.25.

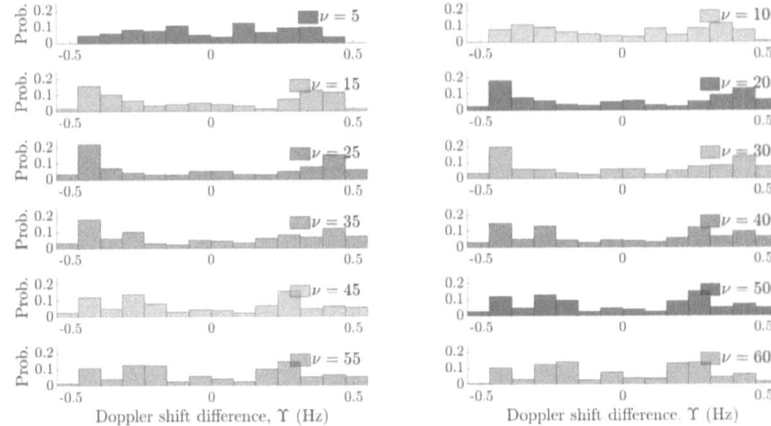

Figure 2.18: A zoomed-in version of Fig. 2.16.

Correlation Between L1 and L2 Pseudorange Errors   In case of NLOS, the pseudorange errors on the two carrier frequencies show a strong linear correlation, see Fig. 2.26. Due to the absence of a direct signal and interference, the pseudorange error will closely follow the reflection delay, regardless of the carrier frequency. However, in case of MP reception, the interference causes the pseudoranges to jump irregularly, depending on the carrier frequency. The MP errors are however in general smaller than the NLOS errors. The SPLOS pseudorange errors are, as expected, all concentrated at zero, and not clearly visible in the figure.

2.10   Discussion

The results on the reflection delay distribution seem to agree with [WCL18], in the sense that they follow a gamma distribution. However, a difference is that [WCL18] found that the scale parameter of the distribution varies between 2 and 3, explained by the hypothesis that the signals are typically reflected two to three times. However, the simulation in Section 2.4 only checks for signals that reflect once, which could be one reason for this difference. Moreover, Shanghai has wide streets with skyscrapers sometimes only on one side, which could also be a reason for the discrepancy. For a quantitive estimation of the fit of the gamma distributions in Fig. 2.11, a statistical analysis is needed. The presented distributions visually fit, however the historgrams could be plotted with other resolutions to get a better of how well the fit gamma distributions generalize.

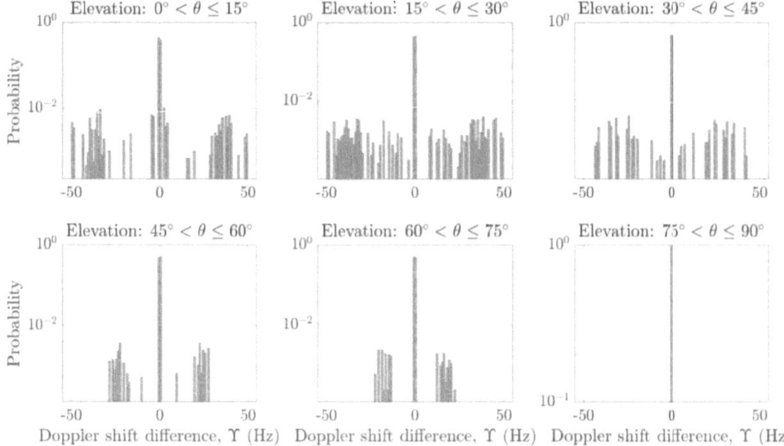

Figure 2.19: A version of Fig. 2.17 where the probability axis is logarithmic, so that the smaller values are clearer.

Method-wise, the ideal situation would be to collect data from several cities, such as New York City, Frankfurt, Chicago, Shanghai, etc., with receivers capable of distinguishing individual reflections with high precision. In this way, it would be possible to analyze which reflection characteristics that remain constant for all types of urban canyons. Another possibility would be to take 3D maps from these urban areas, and import them into the ray tracing simulation, to get a realistic and representative set of geometric configurations. This could also give an idea of how reasonable the choice of a Rice distribution is. Unfortunately, there is no natural law that predicts what a city looks like, the immediate surroundings of the vehicle can switch between tall and low buildings quickly, furthermore the material can switch between, e.g., glass and concrete on short notice. Therefore, simulation is still a very powerful tool to get an understanding of the urban canyon problem in satellite navigation, since the geometric configuration is easy to change. In total, over 20 000 reflections have been considered, so the data sets should be representative of each respective building height. In these simulations, an LHCP rejection value of 3 dB has been used, however one could try other values or even make it elevation-dependent instead.

2.11   Conclusions

In this chapter, a 3D urban area has been combined with a model of electromagnetic wave propagation and a receiver simulation, to get an idea of which distributions the pseudorange error

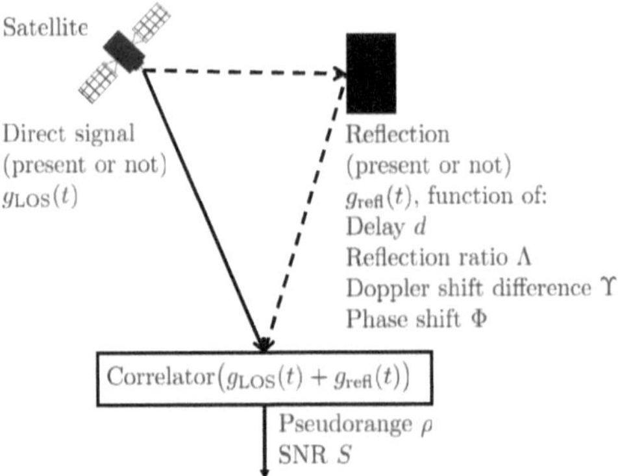

Figure 2.20: The correlator bases the pseudorange on the sum of all received signals (direct and/or reflections).

and its underlying parameters follow. The distribution reflection delay is concentrated at smaller values as the satellite elevation grows, while the RR concentrates around a value of 0.7. Most importantly, the pseudorange error distribution is non-Gaussian, with most values around 0, and with outliers up to several hundred meters. The reflection delays follow a gamma distribution, whose shape parameters is close to the median reflection delay, depending on the urban canyon depth. The number of satellites also closely depends on the urban canyon depth, thus a simple quadratic model can give a prior distribution on the reflection delays, which is useful for MP delay estimation, which will be studied in Chapter 4.

This simulation could also be used to obtain results from non-symmetric urban areas, or to study the temporal evolution of each reflection; how long to they last and how fast to they change? In the future, other, more asymmetric geometric configurations could be simulated, to see if and how the results change. The importance of the building material and window placements could also be studied, since this could cause the RR to rapidly change at high vehicle velocities. The source code for the urban canyon simulation is available at   so that researchers can create their own simulations to try new scenarios.

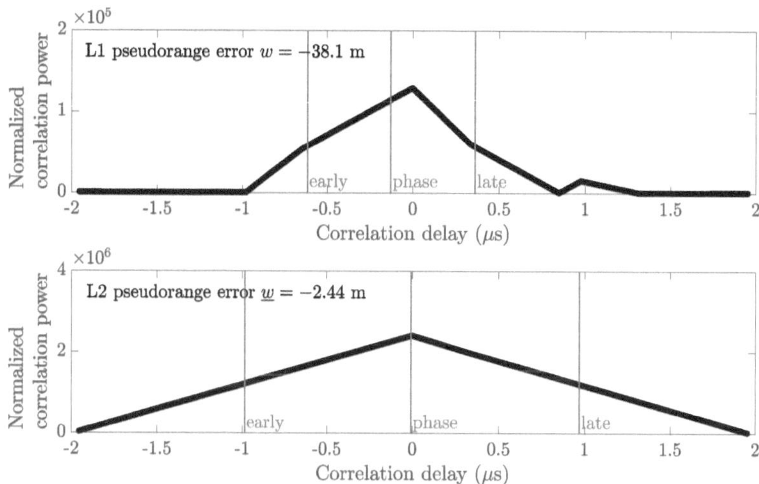

Figure 2.21: The Multipath (MP) reception distorts the correlator output of the L1 and L2 signals, causing pseudorange errors.

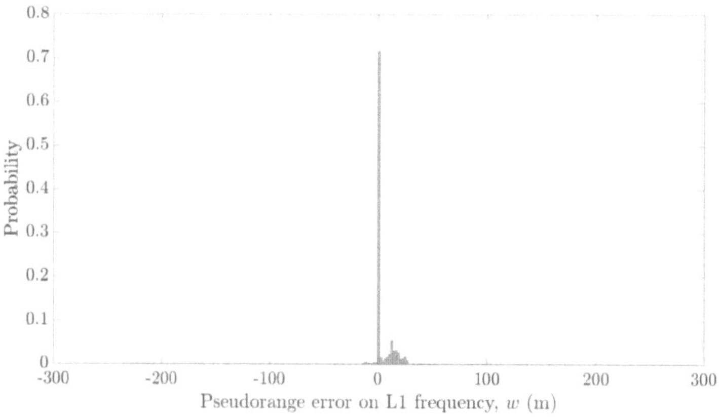

Figure 2.22: For the Global Positioning System (GPS) L1 signal, the pseudorange errors follow a highly non-Gaussian distribution.

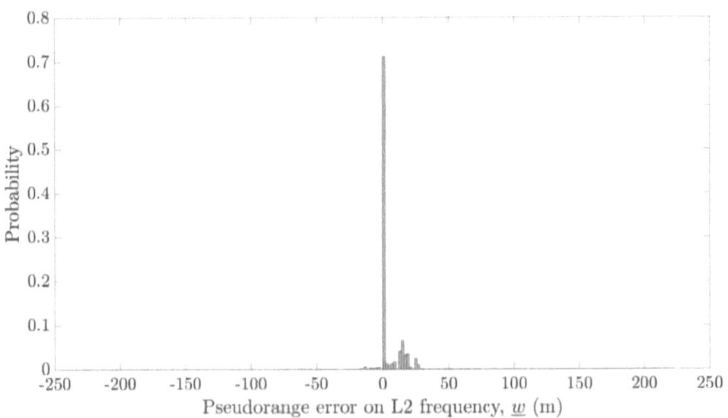

Figure 2.23: For the Global Positioning System (GPS) L2 signal, the pseudorange errors follow a highly non-Gaussian distribution, similarly to the L1 signal of the same system.

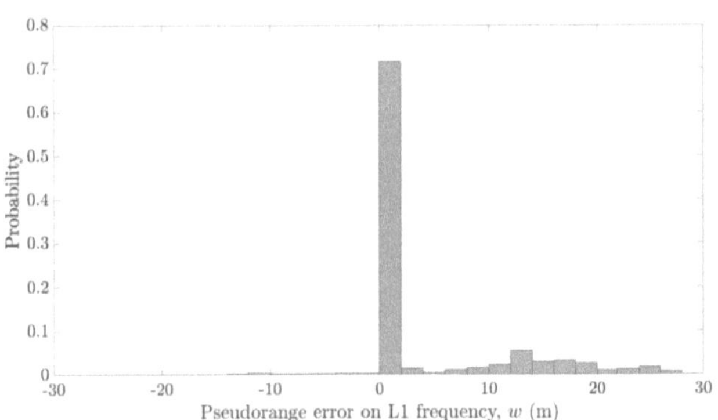

Figure 2.24: A zoomed-in version of Fig. 2.22.

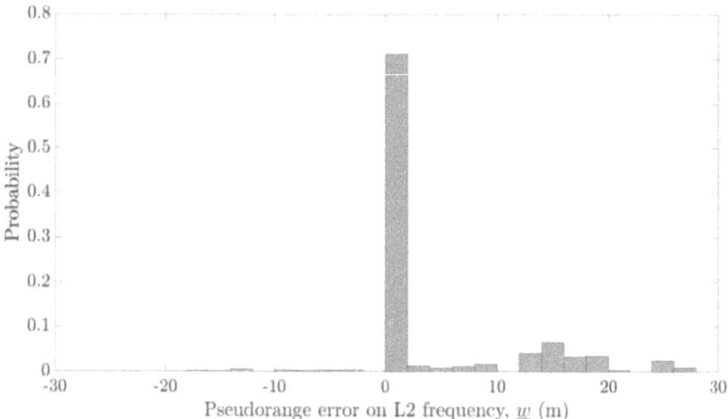

Figure 2.25: A zoomed-in version of Fig. 2.23.

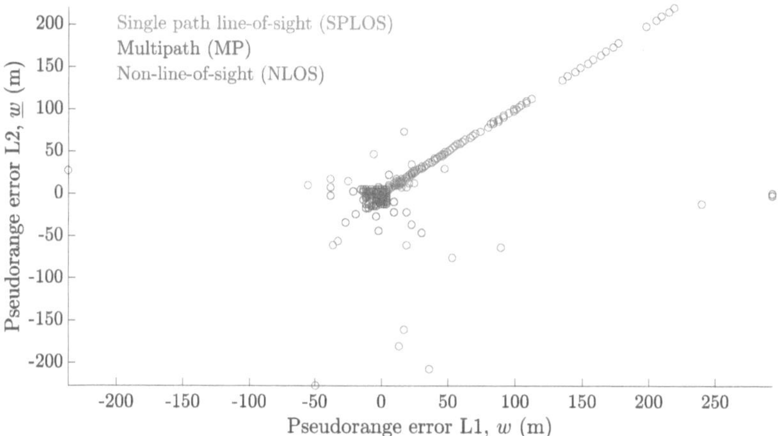

Figure 2.26: The pseudorange errors on the L1 and L2 carrier frequencies show a strong linear correlation in case of Non-Line-of-Sight (NLOS) reception.

Chapter 3

Detection of Reflections for Satellite Selection

The goal in this chapter is to estimate the quality of the pseudorange measurements from each satellite, so that a subset of satellites that results in a better position estimate can be selected (in contrast to naively using all available satellites. This is done using correlator output measured on two carrier frequencies in Section 3.3) and using a combination of pseudorange and SNR measurements on two carrier frequencies in Section 3.4. In urban areas with moderate building heights (Fig. 2.6), or when a receiver works with several GNSS constellations (such as GPS and Galileo), there can still be enough satellites available to compute a position after filtering out the ones influenced by reflections. Under these conditions, reflection detection with satellite selection is a simple approach that can be done using easily available observables that do not require advanced hardware.

> The correlator-based satellite classification method is based on [OBB19], with the addition of the Pearson correlation variant. The dual-frequency satellite selection algorithm is based on [OSBB20].

First, the satellite selection problem is formulated in Section 3.1. Second, related work is discussed in Section 3.2. Third, the dual-frequency correlator-based approach to classification satellite reception is presented in Section 3.3. Fourth, Section 3.4 introduces a satellite selection approach that classifies and prioritizes satellites based on dual-frequency pseudorange and SNR. Finally, a discussion can be found in Section 3.5 and the conclusions are in Section 3.6.

3.1 Problem Formulation

A receiver receives L satellites, indexed by l. Each satellite sends data on two carrier frequencies, with the most important measurement being the pseudorange

$$\rho^l = \sqrt{(r^x - s^{l,x})^2 + (r^y - s^{l,y})^2 + (r^z - s^{l,z})^2} + b + w^l + v_\rho, \tag{3.1}$$

where b is the receiver clock bias in meters, w^l is the error caused by reflections (following the distributions from Section 2.9), and v_ρ is Gaussian measurement noise with zero mean and standard deviation σ_ρ. The variables $s^{l,x}$, $s^{l,y}$, and $s^{l,z}$ represent the ECEF position of the satellite l. The pseudorange is also measured on the second carrier frequency

$$\underline{\rho}^l = \sqrt{(r^x - s^{l,x})^2 + (r^y - s^{l,y})^2 + (r^z - s^{l,z})^2} + b + \underline{w}^l + \underline{v}_\rho, \tag{3.2}$$

where $\underline{w}^l$ is the error caused by reflections, and $\underline{v}_\rho$ is Gaussian measurement noise with zero mean and standard deviation $\underline{\sigma}_\rho$.

The SNR on frequency 1 depends on the satellite elevation θ according to [DRB18]

$$S^l = 3.199\text{e-}5(\theta^l)^3 - 8.1\text{e-}3(\theta^l)^2 + 0.6613\theta^l + 31.38 + v_S. \tag{3.3}$$

The L2 signal is transmitted with 3 dB less power than the L1 signal

$$\underline{S}^l = S^l - 3\,\text{dB} + \underline{v}_S. \tag{3.4}$$

The SNR on both frequencies have Gaussian measurement noise with zero mean and standard deviations σ_S and $\underline{\sigma}_S$, respectively. To obtain the SNR values from a GNSS receiver, one can use the C/N_0, which is the SNR normalized to a bandwidth of 1 Hz. A further analysis of the received C/N_0 for high-sensitive receivers can be found in [WGH05].

Using these input data (pseudoranges and SNR on two frequencies along with the satellite elevations), the goal is to select a subset containing at least four satellites that output pseudoranges with the minimal RMS with respect to the true pseudoranges $\rho_{\text{ref}}^1, \ldots, \rho_{\text{ref}}^i, \ldots, \rho_{\text{ref}}^I$, see Fig. 3.1

$$\epsilon_\rho = \sqrt{\frac{1}{I} \sum_{i=1}^{I} (\rho^i - \rho_{\text{ref}}^i)^2} \tag{3.5}$$

$$I \geq 4.$$

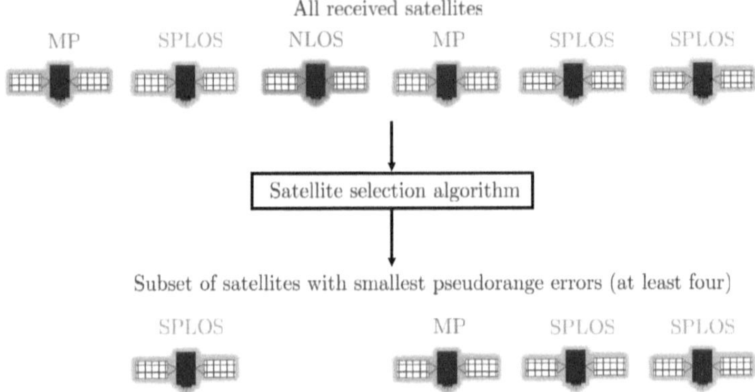

Figure 3.1: The purpose of satellite selection is to exclude the satellites with largest pseudorange errors, while keeping at least four to compute the position.

3.2   Related Work

In this chapter, two concepts are important. First of all, multi-frequency reception will recur throughout the remaining chapters and it is a central theme for this book.

Multi-frequency reception in GNSS has been used for, e.g., general accuracy improvement [KRB04], or to reduce ionospheric errors [SL11], [MPOC11]. It also has applications in detecting MP, e.g., based on the SNR as in [SG16], since MP interference causes variations in the SNR. A review of multi-frequency methods to detect and mitigate reflections can be found in [OBB18].

Secondly, the correlator output contains crucial information about the received signals and if reflections are p resent. This is called post-correlation analysis, and typical receivers only use three correlator points: the early, phase and late correlators. The pseudorange is determined by finding a point where the early and late correlators have about the same correlation power, and it should be low. The pseudorange is then determined by the localization of the phase correlator, who should have a high correlation power there. In case of MP, interference and extra peaks will appear in correlation form, distorting it (see Fig. 2.21), and NLOS can cause the receiver to simply identify the reflection as the direct signal, causing a delay in the p seudorange. Post-correlation can thus detect corrupt correlation forms, for example by analyzing its symmetry [ERSGLS+15]. Another method is the early late phase parameter [MD10b], which analyzes the three correlators to detect MP. This has also been done based on FFT [ADK+16]. Other examples are methods based on deconvolution, such as Projection onto convex sets, [SSL09, DB11]. Further methods, based on filtering are Virtual MP mitigation technique [RC09], the Linear adaptive filter [UP13], and Wide-sense stationary uncorrelated scattering [EA17]. Signal quality monitoring is the concept of analyzing observables related to the GNSS signal, so errors can be detected, including MP. This can also be done based on the correlator output [PALO17]. Another emerging type of methods is to apply machine learning to the correlator output [SBL14, SNA17, LHL$^+$16, MBC20], which is especially interesting for software-defined receivers, since many parameters and raw data are easily accessible.

In summary, minimization of reflection errors in GNSS has previously been done based on multi-frequency reception, including based on SNR on multiple carrier frequencies. It has also been done based on correlator output, however not based on multiple on frequencies, which is the purpose of this chapter.

3.3 Dual-Frequency Correlator-Based Classification of GNSS Signals

One approach to the satellite selection problem is to classify all received satellites according to their reception mode: SPLOS, MP, or NLOS, see Fig. 2.5. Then, assuming that the NLOS pseudorange errors are in general larger than the MP pseudorange errors (as seen in Fig. 2.26), one selects first the SPLOS satellites, then the MP satellites and finally the NLOS satellites. The selection stops when no more SPLOS are available, or when four satellites have been selected if MP or NLOS satellites have to be included.

The correlator output [KH07, p. 65] is crucial for computing the pseudorange, but it also contains information about the MP situation. On one hand, the interference between the direct signal and the reflection under MP will increase or decrease the correlation power and on the other hand, reflections will cause additional peaks in the correlator output to appear, creating asymmetry. The resulting MP correlation power depends on the carrier frequency; it might be constructive on one frequency, while the other is destructive, which is why multi-frequency transmission is interesting for this purpose. Correlator output-based MP mitigation has previously been done with one carrier frequency [ERSGLS$^+$15, MD10b, ADK$^+$16, SSL09, DB11], also in combination with machine learning [LHL$^+$16].

The development and validation of the dual-frequency correlator-based classification method, was done according to Fig. 3.2. The development was done based on a highly controllable reflection scenario created in a GNSS signal generator, while a preliminary validation was done with real satellite data.

Reflection Scenario with Signal Generator A Skydel SDX [Sky19] GNSS signal generator was used to create a basic reflection scenario. This device generates simulated GNSS signals in real-time,

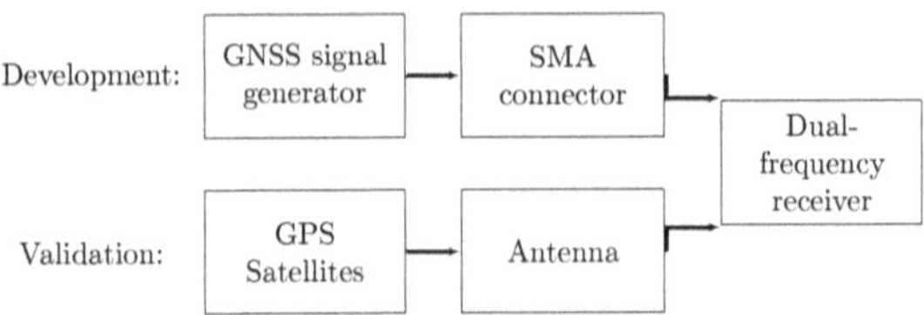

Figure 3.2: The satellite classification method was developed using data from a signal generator, then the method was tested with real satellites. The figure is adopted from [OBB19], ©2019 IEEE.

using the same carrier frequencies as the satellites. Up to three reflections can be added, all with their own delay, power loss, phase shift, and Doppler shift difference.

The reflection scenario consists of 18 reflections, each lasting 1 second and with 1 second of reflection-free data in-between. All reflections were 3 dB weaker than the direct signal ($\Lambda \approx 0.71$) and nine different delays were used (all in meters): 1, 2, 3, 4, 5, 10, 15, 20, 25. The first nine reflections are MP while the following nine reflections are the same without the direct signal, making them NLOS. A Python script switches the reflections on and of in the signal generator. Only the GPS satellite with Pseudorandom Noise (PRN) number 32 was affected by the reflections, however the reflection settings were identical on both carrier frequencies. The simulated vehicle was set to move with a constant speed of 50 km/h in a circle of 1 km radius with its center near the border between the United States and Canada, at the coordinates $\lambda = 45°$, $\phi = -73°$. The reflection scenario is detailed in Table 3.1.

Dual-Frequency Receiver   The generator was connected to a Teseo V from ST Microelectronics [STM19] dual-frequency receiver using an SubMiniature Version A (SMA) cable. The Teseo V can record 10 correlator points, evenly spaced between -1 chip and 1.25 chips. Furthermore, pseudorange, Doppler shift, C/N_0, and carrier phase offset are available parameters. This output is given at a sample rate of 5 Hz, in National Marine Electronics Association (NMEA) format. All output is available on two carrier frequencies; the selected dual-frequency combination was the GPS L1 and L2 signals, since this gave the most available GPS satellites transmitting both frequencies at the time of data collection in October 2018. This is interesting for researching dual-frequency methods, since direct sampling of the signals would require an unrealistic sampling rate near 3 GHz, and result in a mix of signal of all satellites. It is faster to process than Intermediate Frequency (IF) data, and results in realistic data with actual receiver noise. Another advantage is that it can work either with GNSS signal generator data, or (by connecting an antenna) with data from real satellites.

L2 Norm-Based Classification Feature and Algorithm   Two variants of the classification algorithm are presented, each using different features. The first feature is based on the L_2 norm. Before

Table 3.1: The reflection simulation scenario consists of 18 reflections (nine Multipath (MP) and nine Non-Line-of-Sight (NLOS)), with reflection-free reception in-between them.

Duration (s)	Direct signal	Reflection	Delay (m)	Power loss (dB)
240	1	0	—	—
1	1	1	1	3
1	1	0	—	—
1	1	1	2	3
1	1	0	—	—
1	1	1	3	3
1	1	0	—	—
1	1	1	4	3
1	1	0	—	—
1	1	1	5	3
1	1	0	—	—
1	1	1	10	3
1	1	0	—	—
1	1	1	15	3
1	1	0	—	—
1	1	1	20	3
1	1	0	—	—
1	1	1	25	3
1	1	0	—	—
1	0	1	1	3
1	1	0	—	—
1	0	1	2	3
1	1	0	—	—
1	0	1	3	3
1	1	0	—	—
1	0	1	4	3
1	1	0	—	—
1	0	1	5	3
1	1	0	—	—
1	0	1	10	3
1	1	0	—	—
1	0	1	15	3
1	1	0	—	—
1	0	1	20	3
1	1	0	—	—
1	0	1	25	3
120	1	0	—	—

presenting the dual-frequency-based MP and NLOS detection, it is first useful to define the L_2 error norm of the vector $\mathbf{C}$ of length K

$$\|\mathbf{C}\|_2 = \sqrt{\sum_{k=1}^{K} |C_k|^2}. \tag{3.6}$$

Second, a reference correlator output is selected from a reflection-free (SPLOS) environment, see Fig. 3.3. The corresponding correlator outputs from both carrier frequencies $\mathbf{C}_{\text{ref}}$ and $\underline{\mathbf{C}}_{\text{ref}}$ are stored. This represents the expected correlator output under normal conditions, and will be used as a reference when comparing new correlator outputs. It is important that $\mathbf{C}_{\text{ref}}$ is symmetric and that the maximum correlator power corresponds to what is expected from a satellite of that elevation. If no reflection-free environment is available (or if there is no way to detect that the receiver is in a reflection-free environment), then an elevation-based signal power according to [DRB18] could be used. The feature on each frequency is then

$$C = \frac{1}{\sqrt{K}} \|\mathbf{C} - \mathbf{C}_{\text{ref}}\| \tag{3.7}$$

$$\underline{C} = \frac{1}{\sqrt{K}} \|\underline{\mathbf{C}} - \underline{\mathbf{C}}_{\text{ref}}\| \tag{3.8}$$

Third, the classification is done according to Algorithm 1. The intuition behind the classification

---

Algorithm 1 The satellites are classified according to their reception mode, based on correlator output on two frequencies.

---

for all satellites l of L **do**
    $C = \frac{1}{\sqrt{K}} \|\mathbf{C} - \mathbf{C}_{\text{ref}}\|$
    $\underline{C} = \frac{1}{\sqrt{K}} \|\underline{\mathbf{C}} - \underline{\mathbf{C}}_{\text{ref}}\|$
    $C_\Delta = |C - \underline{C}|$
    if $(C < T_C \text{ AND } \underline{C} < T_C)$ **then**
      $E_l = \text{SPLOS}$
    else
      if $C_\Delta > T_\Delta$ **then**
        $E_l = \text{MP}$
      else
        $E_l = \text{NLOS}$
      end if
    end if
end for

---

algorithm is that, in case of MP, the interference between the direct signal and the reflection will change the received correlation power, compared with SPLOS reception. The correlation power will increase in relation to SPLOS in case of constructive interference, and decrease in case of destructive interference. Furthermore, if enough correlation points are available, the secondary correlation peak will cause the received correlator form to differ even more from the expected

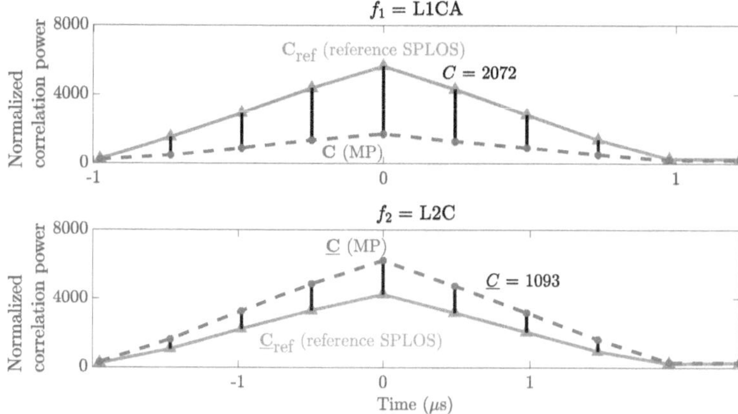

Figure 3.3: To detect Multipath (MP), a reference correlator output is compared to the receiver correlator output on two carrier frequencies. The difference is quantified using the L_2 norm, which will increase when large interference between the direct signal and a reflection is present. The figure is adapted from [OBB19].

SPLOS correlator output. The used hardware with 10 correlator points is not enough for this, it is unlikely that the additional reflection peak is near any of these 10 points. For these reasons, the L_2 is norm suitable to quantify the difference between two correlator forms, since it can both detect differences in correlation power and additional peaks (if the hardware proposes many correlator points). For NLOS reception, no interference is expected, thus the L_2 norm will differ in the same way for both carrier frequencies, making it possible to also identify this reception mode. The threshold would need fine-tuning depending on the receiver, since the correlation power is given normalized, relative to the used receiver.

In Fig. 3.4, the feature on each frequency is visualized during the GNSS signal generator scenario. Based on the signal generator scenario, the thresholds in Algorithm 1 were manually tuned to $T_C = 200$ and $T_\Delta = 150$. A patent for this feature is pending [OB19c].

Pearson Correlation-Based Classification Feature The second variant of the classification algorithm uses a feature that is based on the Pearson correlation coefficient. The previously explained L_2 norm-based feature basically averages the correlator output over all samples, making it highly related to the received signal strength. This is reasonable when only 10 correlator points are available, because it is unlikely that the reflection will be near any of the correlation points. However, with more correlator points, the reflections become more apparent in the correlator output, which makes it relevant to analyze the correlator form point by point. One way to do this is with the

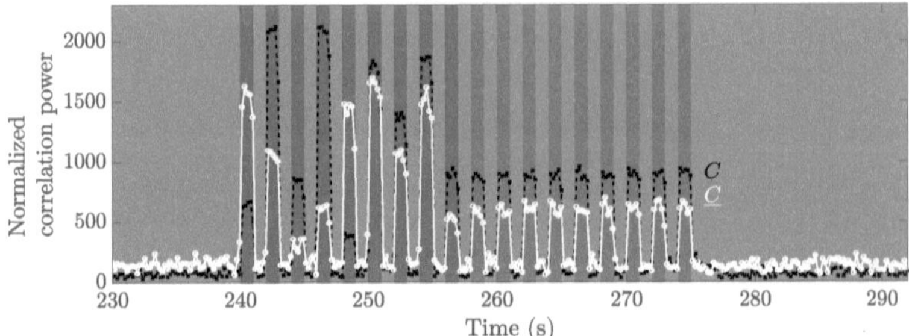

Figure 3.4: The correlator-based feature on two frequencies can detect Multipath (MP) and Non-Line-of-Sight (NLOS) using simple thresholds as in Algorithm 1. The background colors follow Fig. 2.5 and the figure is adapted from [OBB19]. In the blue zones, the interference of Multipath (MP) causes variations in the feature depending on the phase difference between direct signal and reflection. In the red zones, the abscence of interference in Non-Line-of-Sight (NLOS) creates a more regular pattern.

Pearson correlation coefficient, which measures the linear correlation between two vectors of data $\mathbf{X}$ and $\mathbf{Y}$ [DHS01, p. 614]

$$\beta(\mathbf{X}, \mathbf{Y}) = \frac{\sum_{k=1}^{K} (X_k - \mu_{\mathbf{X}})(Y_k - \mu_{\mathbf{Y}})}{\sigma_{\mathbf{X}} \sigma_{\mathbf{Y}}}, \tag{3.9}$$

where

$$\mu_{\mathbf{X}} = \frac{1}{K} \sum_{k=1}^{K} X_k, \tag{3.10}$$

is the arithmetic mean of the vector $\mathbf{X}$ and

$$\sigma_{\mathbf{X}} = \sqrt{\sum_{k=1}^{K} (X_k - \mu_{\mathbf{X}})^2} \tag{3.11}$$

is its standard deviation. If $\mathbf{X}$ and $\mathbf{Y}$ have a perfect positive linear correlation, β will be equal to 1. This can be used to measure the similarity of two signals, and that is how it will be used here.

Depending on the interference between the direct signal and reflections, the received signal strength will increase or decrease the maximal correlation of the received correlator output $\mathbf{C}$. This signal strength difference is represented by scale factor

$$G = \frac{\max(\mathbf{C})}{\max(\mathbf{C}_{\text{ref}})}. \tag{3.12}$$

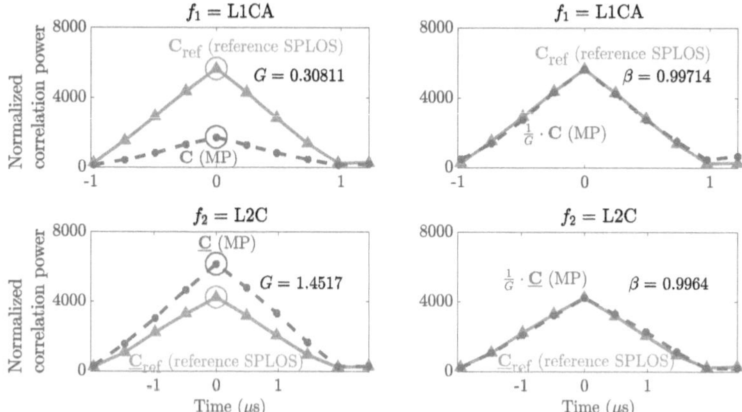

Figure 3.5: As a preparation for computing the features, a scaling factor and the Pearson correlation coefficient between a received correlation form and a reference correlation are computed.

To allow the similarity of the correlator outputs, $\mathbf{C}$ is scaled using this scale factor

$$\mathbf{C}_{\text{scaled}} = \frac{1}{G} \cdot \mathbf{C}. \tag{3.13}$$

Then, the similarity between the correlator outputs is given by

$$\beta(\mathbf{C}, \mathbf{C}_{\text{scaled}}). \tag{3.14}$$

The scaling and Pearson correlation steps are visualized in Fig. 3.5.

Finally, the parameters G and β are combined to a MP and NLOS detection parameter

$$B = \left| \frac{\beta}{G} - 1 \right|. \tag{3.15}$$

This is done since the scaling factor G is expected to increase when reflections are present, while the signal similarity β is expected to decrease. The subtraction of 1 is to center the SPLOS samples around 0. In this way, the feature becomes easier to use for classification purposes. This is done in the same way on the second frequency, giving $\underline{B}$. In this way, the feature varies between 0 and 1, which gives a normalized value for signal classification. Similarly to the feature B, both differences in correlation power and differences caused by additional peaks can be detected in this way. Thus, the C features could be replaced by B in Algorithm 1 (with new thresholds values, since this

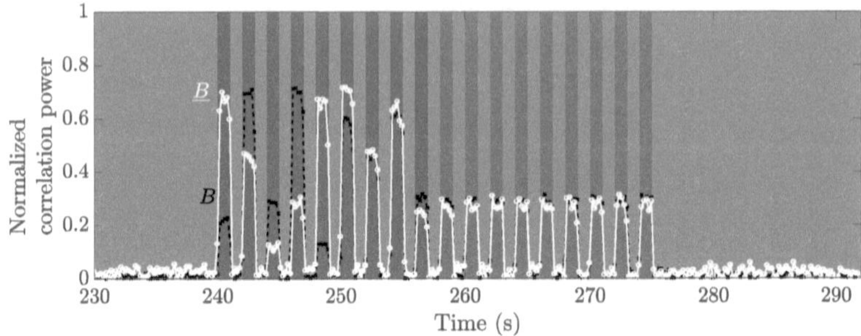

Figure 3.6: The Pearson correlation-based feature varies between 0 and 1 on both frequencies in case of Multipath (MP), but for Non-Line-of-Sight (NLOS) it stays at around 0.3.

feature is normalized). The intuition is similar to the one of the L_2 norm-based classification, with the advantage of having a normalized feature that should be easier to apply to a wide variety of receivers. It could be a disadvantage having to compute the Pearson correlation between correlator outputs with many points however, since this is a complex operation. The feature values during the signal generator simulation are visualized in Fig. 3.6. A patent for this feature is pending [OB19a].

Comparison with State of the Art   The performances of the proposed dual-frequency satellite classification features were compared with two methods from the state of the art: the CMC [KV17], [HC04] and the SNR difference ΔS [SG16], [vH17].

The first, comparison feature, the CMC feature consists of two observables, one for each carrier frequency, MP_1 and MP_2. These two observables compute the difference between the code-based pseudorange and the carrier phase-based pseudorange on two carrier frequencies

$$MP_1 = \rho_1 - \frac{f_1^2 + f_2^2}{f_1^2 - f_2^2}\Psi_1 + \frac{2f_2^2}{f_1^2 - f_2^2}\Psi_2 \tag{3.16}$$

$$MP_2 = \rho_2 - \frac{2f_1^2}{f_1^2 - f_2^2}\Psi_1 + \frac{f_1^2 + f_2^2}{f_1^2 - f_2^2}\Psi_2, \tag{3.17}$$

where ρ_1 and ρ_2 are the code-based pseudorange measurements. When reflections are received, this difference between code and carrier-based measurements is expected to increase, because the extra traveled path will add cycles ι to the carrier phase measurement. The pseudorange based on the carrier phase measurement is then

$$\Psi_1 = \iota_1 \frac{c}{f_1} \tag{3.18}$$

$$\Psi_2 = \iota_2 \frac{c}{f_2}, \tag{3.19}$$

where ι is the carrier phase measurement in cycles.

The second comparison feature is the SNR difference one. It takes the C/N_0 on two carrier frequencies as input parameter, designated as S_1 and S_2, and looks at their difference to detect MP

$$\Delta S = \sqrt{(S_1 - S_2 - S(\theta))^2}. \tag{3.20}$$

The variable $S(\theta)$ is the expected C/N_0 in an environment free of reflection and signal interference, as a function of the satellite elevation angle θ in degrees

$$S(\theta) = 2 + 0.098\theta - 0.0011\theta^2 + 2.8e^{-6}\theta^3. \tag{3.21}$$

The values S_1 and S_2 are obtained by reading the NMEA log of the Teseo V receiver on each frequency, respectively. The cofficients of (3.21) are derived from data acquisition in a low MP environment using a Leica Viva GS15 geodetic GNSS receiver [SG16].

For the comparison, two binary classification metrics, the Area under the Receiver Operating Characteristic (AUROC) [GS66] and the absolute Fisher Score F [DHS01] are used. The first metric, is based on the Receiver Operating Characteristic (ROC), which is a common way of evaluating detection methods. To obtain a ROC curve, a simple threshold-based classification is done. This threshold is varied, from the lowest value of the feature to the highest value, in a given amount of steps. For each threshold step, the True Positive Rate (TPR) and the False Positive Rate (FPR) are computed, which are correctly classified positives among all positives, and the falsely classified positives among all negatives, respectively. A plot of the TPR against the FPR gives the ROC curve, where a feature that has a low performance in threshold-based classification will follow the diagonal closely, resulting in an area under it, AUROC, close to 0.5. On the other hand, a feature with a high detection performance will stay close to the upper left corner, resulting in an AUROC close to 1.

The second metric, the absolute Fisher score, will increase when a feature has a high inter-class difference (thus, the feature values differ between two classes, such as SPLOS and MP). The metric also increases if the intra-class difference is low, meaning that the values within the same should stay somewhat constant. The absolute Fisher score is computed as

$$F = \frac{|(\mu_1 - \mu_2)|}{\sqrt{\sigma_1^2 + \sigma_2^2}}, \tag{3.22}$$

where μ_c is the mean across all values belonging to a class c and σ_c is the standard deviation across the class c.

The two presented metrics work only for binary classification, thus the three class problem (SPLOS versus MP versus NLOS) cannot be analyzed in this way. Instead, three two-class problems are defined and analyzed:

1. SPLOS versus MP,

2. SPLOS versus NLOS,

3. SPLOS versus (MP or NLOS).

In summary, all three classification problems above have been analyzed using the two metrics, for five features (the proposed novel methods and two from the state of the art). Of these three features, two result in one variable per frequency, thus the results of seven features are presented in total.

The results can be found in Fig. 3.7 and Fig. 3.8, where it can be seen that the proposed methods work better than the state of the art, regardless of how the classification scenario is defined. Furthermore, the Pearson correlation-based variants B and $\underline{B}$ have a slight advantage over the L_2 norm-based ones, C and $\underline{C}$.

Preliminary Validation of L2-Based Classification with Satellite Data To get an impression of the performance of the MP and NLOS detection in real environments with signals from real satellites, test drives were done in two environments: the A7 highway in central Germany and in the city center of Frankfurt am Main, see Fig. 3.9 and Fig. 3.10. No hardware to record the ground truth on reflections was available, so the results are simply the detections made based on real input data, without being able to verify if they are correct. Despite this, we can see that more MP is detected in the Frankfurt environment than on the highway. The MP detected at around 70 seconds on the highway could be a reflection on an overtaken truck. For the test drive, the thresholds of Algorithm 1 were adapted to $T_C = 1300$ and $T_\Delta = 100$. The first part of the Frankfurt test drives is static, thus the feature is reacting to the slow movement of the satellites.

3.4 Dual-Frequency Satellite Selection Algorithm

In this section, Algorithm 1 is extended so that each satellite is given a priority in addition to being classified, which makes satellite selection possible. The previously explained correlator-based features scale well with complex hardware that outputs many correlator points, but for simpler receivers one can use the more common SNR parameter, which however is not as rich in information. For these reasons, the satellite selection method in this algorithm is based on the SNR.

The dual-frequency satellite selection procedure is detailed in Algorithm 2. The idea is that, first,

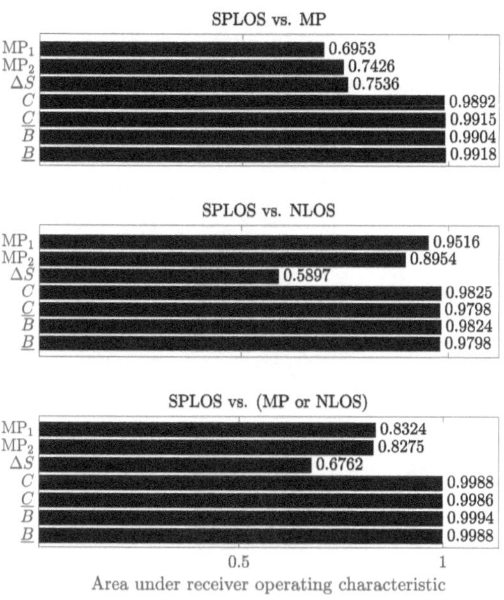

Figure 3.7: According to the Area under the Receiver Operating Characteristic (AUROC) metric, the proposed dual-frequency based features consistently detect Multipath (MP) and Non-Line-of-Sight (NLOS) better than three other features, taken from the state of the art. The figures are adapted from [OBB19].

the two pseudoranges are compared to identify SPLOS, they are expected to be very close in this case (only measurement noise should cause differences). In case of MP the pseudoranges differ due to interference. To distinguish SPLOS from NLOS, the SNR on both frequencies is also compared, it should be around 3 dB (since the L2 signals is transmitted at 3 dB less power for GPS). NLOS is then classified if the SNR on frequency 1 is close to what is expected according to an elevation-based model [DRB18], because in absence of interference mainly the satellite elevation will influence the SNR. These satellites are then given a priority number that is inversely proportional to their SNR, so that the strongest NLOS will be selected before the weaker ones. All other satellites are classified as MP, with the absolute pseudorange different as priority number. After the classification and prioritization of all satellites is done, they are selected so that all SPLOS are selected first, then if four satellites are not reached, the selection continues according to first MP and then NLOS, with the priority described as above. The thresholds were tuned according

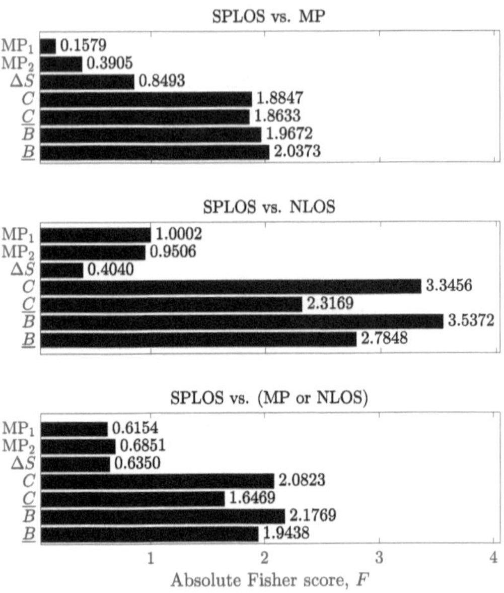

Figure 3.8: According to the Fisher score metric, the proposed dual-frequency based features consistently detect Multipath (MP) and Non-Line-of-Sight (NLOS) better than three other features, taken from the state of the art. The figures are adapted from [OBB19].

to the urban canyon simulation in Section 5.6: $T_S = 0.5\,\mathrm{dB}$, $T_\rho = 1\,\mathrm{m}$ (between w^l and v_ρ) and $T_\theta = 4\,\mathrm{dB}$. A patent for this satellite selection procedure is pending [OB20a].

3.5 Discussion

In this chapter, we have seen methods to classify the reception modes based on correlator output, and based on pseudoranges and SNR. The correlator-based features require receivers that output rawer data, however they have good potential to scale well as more correlator points are available. The pseudorange and SNR-based version can be applied to most commercially based receivers, since the output parameters are typically available. The results in this chapter are based on a reflection scenario created with a GNSS signal generator, measured by a dual-frequency receiver that is a prototype for the mass-market. A preliminary validation based on real data (that is, however, missing a ground truth on the reflections) shows that the signal classification might work

Figure 3.9: According to the Fisher score metric, the proposed dual-frequency based features consistently detect Multipath (MP) and Non-Line-of-Sight (NLOS) better than three other features, taken from the state of the art. The figures are adapted from [OBB19].

well also in a real urban canyon. Thus, Algorithm 1 is promising for real-life applications.

Concerning the methods used in this chapter, ideally the reflections in Frankfurt should be recorded with a receiver that can record reflections, and decide the reception mode. This way, a high-quality validation of the method in real urban canyons could be done. The reflection scenario in the GNSS signal generator uses a combination of common reflections, but the simulation in Chapter 2 could also be used to generate more representative reflections, with realistic dynamics. The NMEA data format has limited precision, however the correlator output data are recorded using private messages which are more flexible. Re

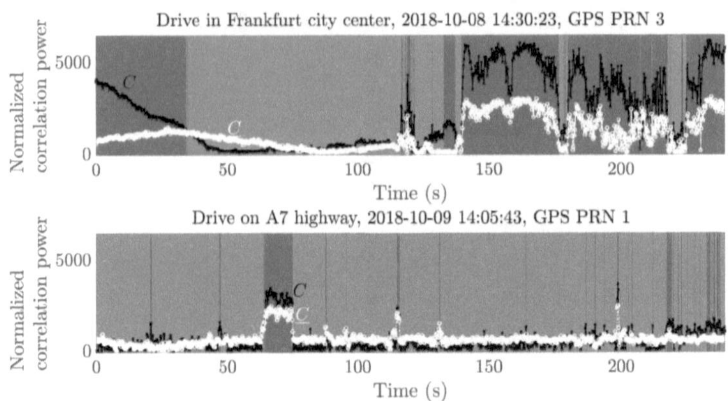

Figure 3.10: The dual-frequency feature detects significantly more Multipath (MP) in the urban environment (upper figures) than on the highway (lower figures). Both figures are adapted from [OBB19] and the satellite photos are from [Goo19].

3.6 Conclusions

In this chapter, we have seen two algorithms that approach navigation in urban areas by classifying and ranking satellites, depending on how large the pseudorange errors of the satellites are. Both algorithms use dual-frequency observables as input, the first one a 10-point correlator output and the second one combines pseudoranges, SNR and satellite elevation. All of these only require a dual-frequency receiver, the input variables themselves are parameters that standard receivers typically record. If few correlator points are available, MP can still be detected, since the correlator power will be reduced or increased by the interference, but if a large amount of correlator points are available (such as in a software-defined receiver), individual reflections can be identified and removed.

The results are based on a combination of all three main tools of GNSS research: simulations, signal generator data, and data from real satellites. This shows good potential for implementing the proposed satellite selection algorithms in real receivers, however the validation with real satellites should be done more extensively and with an accurate ground truth on the reception modes.

We have supposed that the selected subset of satellites with minimal errors from reflections will lead to better positioning, however this ignores the fact that the satellite geometry also influences the accuracy of the position. Chapter 5 is dedicated to evaluating the positioning performance by combining the satellite subsets using an EKF.

Algorithm 2 .

> **for all** satellites l of L **do**
>   **if** $|\rho^l - \underline{\rho}^l| < T_\rho$ AND $|S^l - \underline{S}^l - 3\,\mathrm{dB}| < T_S$ **then**
> $E_l = \mathrm{SPLOS}$
> $E_l^{\mathrm{prio}} = 0$
>   **else if** $S_\theta^l = 3.199\text{e-}5(\theta^l)^3 - 8.1\text{e-}3(\theta^l)^2 + 0.6613\theta_l + 31.38 - S^l > T_\theta$ **then**
> $E_l = \mathrm{NLOS}$
> $E_l^{\mathrm{prio}} = \frac{1}{S^l}$
>   **else**
> $E_l = \mathrm{MP}$
> $E_l^{\mathrm{prio}} = |\rho^l - \underline{\rho}^l|$
>   **end if**
> **end for**
> select all satellites belonging to SPLOS
> **while** number of selected satellites $I < 4$ AND all MP satellites not selected **do**
>   select one MP satellite (lowest E_l^{prio}-values first)
> **end while**
> **while** number of selected satellites < 4 AND all NLOS satellites not selected **do**
>   select one NLOS satellite (lowest E_l^{prio}-values first)
> **end while**
> Output the I selected satellites

In the future, combinations other than the L1 and L2C signals could be considered, including, e.g., combinations with the L5 signals. Furthermore, squaring loss [SMMB07] could be take into consideration.

Chapter 4

Mitigation of Multipath

In the case of MP reception, the LOS signal is still present, meaning that the essential ranging information is still received. In this chapter, a method to mitigate MP is presented. The additional delay of the reflection with respect to the direct signal is estimated by analyzing the signal power on multiple carrier frequencies. In contrast to detection of reflections and satellite selection (Chapter 3), reflection delay estimation has the possibility to correct the pseudorange measurements of satellites that are influenced by reflections, thus it is useful in areas where few satellites are available, such as a deep urban canyon.

> This chapter is based on [OBB20a], with the addition of including a prior distribution and more details on the distribution of the signal power measurement noise.

First, the problem of MP delay estimation is formulated in Section 4.1. Second, related work is presented in Section 4.2. Third, Section 4.3 explains how the problem can be approached with ML estimation. Fourth, the prior gamma distribution from Section 2.6 is used in Section 4.4. Fifth, a simulation with different levels of measurement noise is explained in Section 4.5 and its results are presented in Section 4.6. Finally, Section 4.7 gives a discussion while Section 4.8 concludes the chapter.

4.1 Problem Formulation

A situation of MP is considered, see Fig. 2.5. It is supposed that a method to classify the reception mode of the signal is available, e.g., the correlator-based approach described in Section 3.3. Thus, it is possible to distinguish MP from NLOS or SPLOS. Since MP reception always includes an LOS signal and at least one reflection, these signals will interfere at the receiver (see Fig. 4.1), creating variations in the received SNR. Since the SNR is easily available on each frequency, we want to use these measurements to estimate the reflection delay. To begin with, a model of the signal power is

"

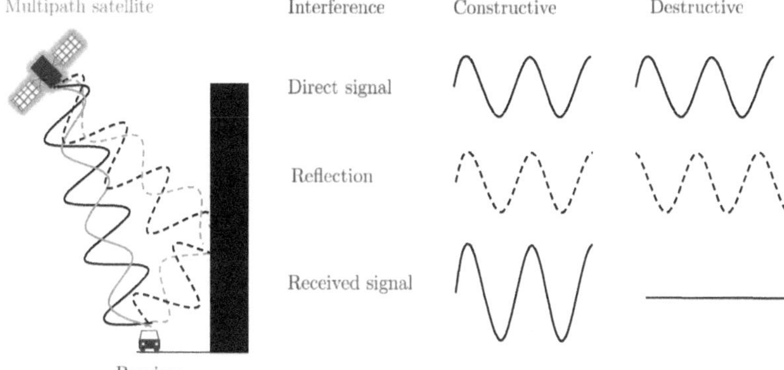

Figure 4.1: Under Multipath (MP) reception, the direct signal and the reflection interfere at the receiver, creating variations in the signal power. This interference pattern is different for each carrier frequency.

needed. For a given reflection scenario, this receiver input power follows a simple rule depending on the frequency. We will use the two-ray signal model described by (2.24), which consists of a direct signal

$$g_{\text{LOS}}(t) = \sqrt{2P_{\text{LOS}}}\cos(2\pi f_n t),\tag{4.1}$$

and one reflection

$$g_{\text{refl}}(t) = \sqrt{2P_{\text{LOS}}}\Lambda\cos(2\pi f_n t + \zeta).\tag{4.2}$$

The difference in phase between direct signal and reflection is

$$\zeta = \frac{2\pi f_n d}{c} + \Phi,\tag{4.3}$$

while the signal power of the summed signal $g(t) = g_{\text{LOS}}(t) + g_{\text{refl}}(t)$ is

$$P(d, \Lambda, P_{\text{LOS}}, f_n) = \lim_{T\to\infty}\frac{1}{2T}\int_{-T}^{T} g^2(t)dt = \lim_{T\to\infty}\frac{1}{2T}\int_{-T}^{T}(g_{\text{LOS}}(t) + g_{\text{refl}}(t))^2 dt =$$

$$\lim_{T\to\infty}\frac{1}{2T}\int_{-T}^{T}\left(\sqrt{2P_{\text{LOS}}}\left(\cos\left(2\pi(f_n + f_{\text{D}}^{\text{LOS}})t\right) + \Lambda\cos\left(2\pi(f_n + f_{\text{D}}^{\text{refl}})(t + \frac{d}{c}) + \Phi\right)\right) + v_g\right)^2 dt.\tag{4.4}$$

Four assumptions are made. First, as presented in Section 2.7, the phase shift of all reflections was equal to π radians, so the first assumption is that the phase change of the reflection itself is constant $\Phi = \pi$. The complete phase change of the received signal is then a combination of Φ and the phase changed caused by the reflection delay. Second, the Doppler shift difference of the reflection is typically a few Hz, as seen in Section 2.8, which is small compared to the typical Doppler shift in the kHz range (thus, $f_D^{\text{refl}} \approx f_D^{\text{LOS}}$), see also Fig. 1.7. As a consequence, it is assumed that the carrier frequencies of the direct signal and the reflection are the same. The third assumption is that the power of the direct signal, P_{LOS}, is known. It can estimated as a function of satellite elevation [GJRS13], or measured in a reflection-free environment, based on, e.g., the correlator output [OBB19]. Fourth, the noise v_g is ignored at the integral level, it will modeled as signal power measurement noise, introduced in Section 4.3. The signal power P of the summed signal in (2.24) is then

$$
\begin{aligned}
P(d, \Lambda, P_{\text{LOS}}, f_n) &= \lim_{T \to \infty} \frac{1}{2T} \int_{-T}^{T} \left(\sqrt{2P_{\text{LOS}}} \left(\cos\left(2\pi f_n t\right) + \Lambda \cos\left(2\pi f_n \left(t + \frac{d}{c}\right) + \pi\right) \right) \right)^2 dt = \\
&\lim_{T \to \infty} \frac{2P_{\text{LOS}}}{2T} \int_{-T}^{T} \cos^2(2\pi f_n t) dt + \lim_{T \to \infty} \frac{2P_{\text{LOS}}}{2T} \int_{-T}^{T} 2\cos(2\pi f_n t)\Lambda \cos\left(2\pi f_n t(t + \frac{d}{c})\right) dt + \\
&\lim_{T \to \infty} \frac{2P_{\text{LOS}}}{2T} \int_{-T}^{T} \Lambda^2 \cos^2\left(2\pi f_n (t + \frac{d}{c}) + \pi\right) dt = 2P_{\text{LOS}}\left(\frac{1}{2} - \Lambda \cos(2\pi f_n \frac{d}{c}) + \Lambda^2\right) = \\
&\qquad\qquad P_{\text{LOS}}\left(1 + \Lambda^2 - 2\Lambda \cos\left(\frac{2\pi f_n d}{c}\right)\right). \quad (4.5)
\end{aligned}
$$

The first term of the sum represents the LOS signal, the second the reflection, while the third term stems from the interference between the two signals, with a periodic dependence on the carrier frequency. Given signal power measurements at multiple carrier frequencies, the goal is to estimate the MP reflection delay as defined in (2.7) and in Fig. 2.8. When the reflection delay is known, the inverse MP error envelope of the correlator function [IB03] can be used to compute the pseudorange error, which can finally correct the pseudorange measurement.

4.2   Related Work

Numerous SNR-based methods for detection and mitigation of reflection errors exist. If the receiver is stationary, it is possible to filter SNR with respect to time [BFK$^+$97, ACM96, CA98], so that the reflection delay is estimated. As of 2020, dual and triple-frequency GNSS transmission [OBB18] is reaching the mass market, introducing new information diversity. This is interesting for MP mitigation because different carrier frequencies will fit a different number of wavelengths inside the extra traveled, which influences the received signal power and as a consequence, the SNR on each frequency. This adds new potential to the previously mentioned methods, which do not utilize multi-frequency information. However, SNR-based multi-frequency methods to detect reflections already exist [SG16, GJRS13, vH17, OBB19]. The detection can then be used to exclude or down-weight the reflection-influenced satellites, but this requires a sufficient (at least four) number of error-free satellites. Therefore, it is more interesting to approach the problem with mitigation, meaning that the satellite measurements are corrected instead of excluded. Examples of methods for mitigation of MP errors by estimating the reflection delay are the least squares [MVT94], maximum likelihood [Fuc97, LK06, XHH12, Asl13] methods, and Bayesian filtering [LKR08]. These are however only based on data from one carrier frequency, thus the potential of multi-frequency for reflection delay estimation needs further exploration.

Channel models of SNR have already been studied in the area of wireless communications [CCS11]. This area, however, focuses on reducing communication errors instead of measuring the distance between a transmitter and a receiver, as in GNSS. Furthermore, the concept of orthogonal frequency division multiplexing [Cha66], is an important related method, that uses carefully selected orthogonal frequencies, to reduce communication errors under MP. Another related concept is filter bank multicarrier modulation [ZL08], but it supposes that all carrier frequencies can be selected, unlike what is possible for GNSS.

4.3 Maximum Likelihood Estimation

The signal power is measured at each frequency n, we will consider the typical triple-frequency ($N = 3$) combination of GPS and Galileo

1. $f_1 = 1.5754\,\text{GHz}$ (GPS L1 or Galileo E1),

2. $f_2 = 1.2276\,\text{GHz}$ (GPS L2 or Galileo E5b),

3. $f_3 = 1.1765\,\text{GHz}$ (GPS L5 or Galileo E5a).

Noise Characterization The measured signal power $\hat{P}_n$ differs from the true signal power $P(\bar{d}, \bar{\Lambda}, P_{\text{LOS}}, f_n)$ at the true values $d = \bar{d}$ and $\Lambda = \bar{\Lambda}$

$$\hat{P}_n = P(\bar{d}, \bar{\Lambda}, P_{\text{LOS}}, f_n) + v_{S,n}. \tag{4.6}$$

This is due to the signal power measurement noise, $v_{S,n}$. To characterize this measurement noise, the Skydel SDX GNSS signal generator [Sky19] was connected to an STMicroelectronics Teseo V dual-frequency receiver [STM19]. This hardware simulation used the GPS L1 and L2 signals. The simulation consisted of nine reflections, each lasting 1 second. The dual-frequency sampled the correlator output at 5 Hz. The reflection delay $\bar{d}$ varied from 1 m to 25 m, with the following values: 1, 2, 3, 4, 5, 10, 15, 20, and 25 m. All reflections were 3 dB weaker than the direct signal, giving $\bar{\Lambda} = 10^{\frac{-3\,\text{dB}}{20\,\text{dB}}} \approx 0.71$. This is the MP part of the simulation described in Table 3.1.

As previously mentioned, the signal power can be estimated using observables such as the C/N_0 or the SNR. Another possibility is to base it upon the correlator output, which is also highly sensitive to signal interference (Section 3.3), which is the case in this chapter.

The signal power was based on the average of an 10-point correlator output as in Section 3.3, giving the variables C for the L1 frequency and $\underline{C}$ for the L2 frequency. These are, however averaged correlation powers that are normalized to the receiver, thus they need a transformation be relatable to the signal power described in the model (4.5). For this, the linear transformations

$$\hat{P}_1^{\text{corr}} = 1.99C + 6.71\text{e-}4, \tag{4.7}$$

on the L1 frequency, and between $\underline{C}$ and $\bar{P}_2$ on the L2 frequency

$$\hat{P}_2^{\text{corr}} = 1.93\underline{C} + 8.83\text{e-}4, \tag{4.8}$$

were fitted, for $P_{\text{LOS}} = 1$. The fitted linear squares parameters are close on both frequencies, indicating that the transformation could be valid regardless of the carrier frequency. The mean absolute error between the transformed measurement and the model is

$$\sum_i^I |\hat{P}_{1,i}^{\text{corr}} - \bar{P}_{1,i}| = 0.0474, \tag{4.9}$$

for L1 and

$$\sum_i^I |\hat{P}_{2,i}^{\text{corr}} - \bar{P}_{2,i}| = 0.0370, \tag{4.10}$$

for L2.

The results of the least squares fit can be found in Fig. 4.2, for all delays on both frequencies. First, it is interesting to note how the signal power based on correlator output is typically completely different for the two carrier frequencies, even though the reflection delay and RR is the same. This is due to the aforementioned interference. The correlator output was sampled at 5 Hz and each reflection lasts 1 s, thus one could expect five data points per reflection. However, only four are present, since the GNSS signal generator and the dual-frequency receiver have no external synchronization signal. Thus, only the four middle samples are included, to avoid including data from points in time where the reflection scenario switches.

Subsequently, a Lilliefors test [Con98] was done, supporting (with a p-value of 0.5) the hypothesis that the measurement noise follows a Gaussian distribution (mean $9.41\text{e-}17\,\text{V}^2$ and standard deviation $\sigma_{S,n} = 4.28\text{e-}2\,\text{V}^2$).

Thus, we assume an additive white Gaussian signal power measurement noise with standard deviation $\sigma_{S,n}$

$$v_{S,n} \sim \mathcal{N}(0,\, \sigma_{S,n}^2). \tag{4.11}$$

By combining (4.6) and (4.11),

$$\hat{P}_n \sim \mathcal{N}\big(P(\bar{d}, \bar{\Lambda}, P_{\text{LOS}}, f_n),\, \sigma_{S,n}^2\big), \tag{4.12}$$

is obtained.

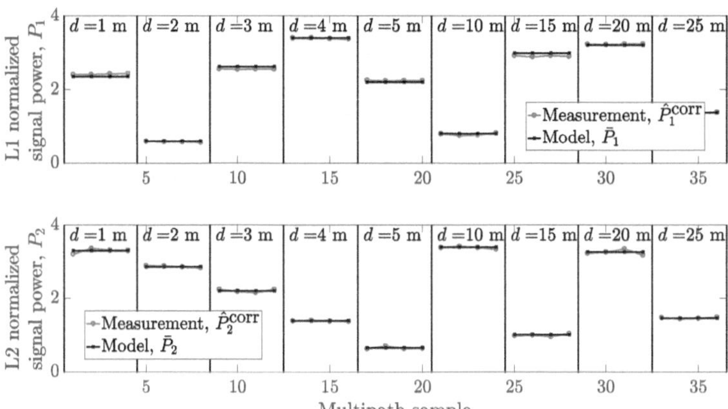

Figure 4.2: Signal power measurements can be obtained by averaging and transforming the correlator output with a linear model.

Likelihood Function By making the assumption that the measurements on each frequency are independent, we can form the likelihood Lik of the parameters d and Λ, given the measurements $\hat{P}_1, \ldots, \hat{P}_N$

$$\text{Lik}(d, \Lambda | \hat{P}_1, \ldots, \hat{P}_N) = \prod_{n=1}^{N} \frac{1}{\sigma_{S,n}\sqrt{2\pi}} \exp\left(-\frac{\left(\hat{P}_n - P(d, r, \Lambda, f_n)\right)^2}{2\sigma_{S,n}^2}\right) \tag{4.13}$$

In this way, the goal of estimating d can be seen as an ML problem, where the also Λ needs to be estimated. We seek the values of d and Λ that maximize the likelihood of observing the measurements $\hat{P}_1, \ldots, \hat{P}_N$

$$(\hat{d}, \hat{\Lambda}) = \underset{d,\Lambda}{\arg\max} \left(\text{Lik}(d, \Lambda | \hat{P}_1, \ldots, \hat{P}_N)\right) =$$

$$\underset{d,\Lambda}{\arg\max} \prod_{n=1}^{N} \frac{1}{\sigma_{S,n}\sqrt{2\pi}} \exp\left(-\frac{\left(\hat{P}_n - P(d, \Lambda, P_{\text{LOS}}, f_n)\right)^2}{2\sigma_{S,n}^2}\right). \tag{4.14}$$

To simplify, the log-likelihood is applied. If all $\sigma_{S,n}$ are equal (meaning that the measurement noise on each frequency has the same standard deviation), the log-likelihood becomes

$$(\hat{d}, \hat{\Lambda}) = \underset{d,\Lambda}{\arg\min} \sum_{n=1}^{N} \left(\hat{P}_n - P(d, \Lambda, P_{\text{LOS}}, f_n)\right)^2. \tag{4.15}$$

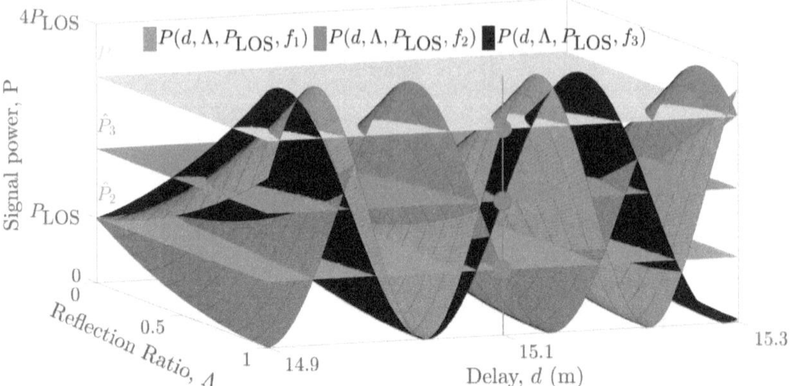

Figure 4.3: By identifying where the signal power measurements (planes) intersect the signal power function surfaces, the reflection delay (15.1 m) can be identified. The figure is adapted from [OBB20a].

In case of differing $\sigma_{S,n}$, a weighted solution can be done instead.

Since both the delay and the RR need to be estimated, a minimum of two carrier frequencies are required, $N \geq 2$.

The signal power on three frequencies is visualized in Fig. 4.3. A reflection with a delay of $\bar{d} = 15.1\,\mathrm{m}$ and RR $\bar{\Lambda} = 1$ is present, and signal power measurements intersect the signal power functions at the magenta circles. The magenta dashed line indicates the introduced delay and RR. In case of the completely destructive interference, the power function P reaches a minimum at 0 signal power, with the phase difference between direct signal and reflection being $\zeta = 2\pi k$, where k is an even integer, and $\Lambda = 1$. Completely constructive interference gives the maximal value of P, $4P_{\mathrm{LOS}}$, where $\zeta = 2\pi(k+1)$ and $\Lambda = 1$. Furthermore, $P(d, \Lambda = 0, P_{\mathrm{LOS}}, f_n) = P_{\mathrm{LOS}}$, which means that when the RR is 0, the reflection has no power, and the power of the received signal is simply the power of the direct signal.

4.4 Prior Reflection Delay Distribution

In Section 2.6, a method to estimate the prior distribution using the number of satellites was presented. According to 2.8, a prior Gamma distribution where the shape parameter depends on the number of satellites L is then obtained. If this prior distribution is included, the likelihood function is transformed to

$$\text{Lik}(d, \Lambda | \hat{P}_1, \ldots, \hat{P}_N, L) =$$

$$\text{Gamma}(\hat{d}_m = -0.23L^2 + 5.08L - 4.08, 1) \prod_{n=1}^{N} \frac{1}{\sigma_{S,n}\sqrt{2\pi}} \exp\left(-\frac{\left(\hat{P}_n - P(d, r, \Lambda, f_n)\right)^2}{2\sigma_{S,n}^2}\right). \quad (4.16)$$

In this situation, the log-likelihood is of little help, and a numerical search is done directly within the multiplied likelihood

$$(\hat{d}, \hat{\Lambda}) = \arg\max_{d, \Lambda}$$

$$\text{Gamma}(\hat{d}_m = -0.23L^2 + 5.08L - 4.08, 1) \prod_{n=1}^{N} \frac{1}{\sigma_{S,n}\sqrt{2\pi}} \exp\left(-\frac{\left(\hat{P}_n - P(d, r, \Lambda, f_n)\right)^2}{2\sigma_{S,n}^2}\right). \quad (4.17)$$

As stated in Section 2.6, this model is only valid for GPS, the coefficients of the polynomial would have to be adapted for multi-constellation receivers, since more satellites are available in that case. In the ray tracing simulation, around 8 satellites were received on average.

The multiplication of the likelihoods is visualized in Fig. 4.4. The true reflection delay in this example is $17.53\,\text{m}$, marked by the dashed magenta line. Other settings are $\Lambda = 0.8$ and $\sigma = 50\,\text{mV}^2$. When only frequency 1 is used, the delay cannot be identified, due to the periodicity of the P function. When two frequencies are used, a peak is seen around the correct delay, but is not the one with the highest likelihood, several false peaks are larger (this is caused by the relatively high measurement noise). With three frequencies, not many peaks remain, however the correct delay still cannot be identified. By also multiplying with the prior gamma distribution, the correct delay can be identified. Thus, if a PDF that roughly represents the reflection delays is available, it can be combined with the triple-frequency signal-power based method for improved dleay estimation.

4.5 Simulation with Multi-Frequency Reflection Delay Estimation

To evaluate the performance of the MP delay estimation, a simulation was setup, containing all possible of delays from 0 m to 29.3 m (in steps of 1 mm), RR values Λ from 0 to 1 (in steps of 0.1), and three values of the signal power measurement noise standard deviation: $\sigma_S = 1\text{e-}3\,\text{V}^2$, $\sigma_S = 2\text{e-}3\,\text{V}^2$ and $\sigma_S = 5\text{e-}3\,\text{V}^2$. These three σ_S values represent three different receivers, with different precisions in signal power measurement.

As performance metric, the RMS delay estimation is used, since a simulation is repeated for M

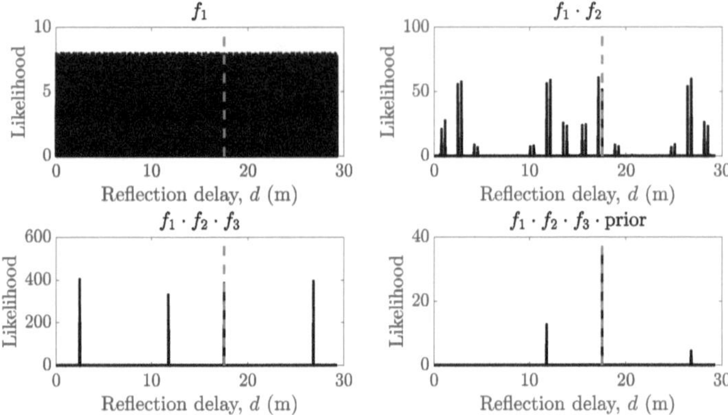

Figure 4.4: By multiplying the likelihood functions of three frequencies with the prior distribution, the correct reflection delay (magenta line) can be identified, in spite of high signal power measurement noise.

Monte Carlo runs

$$d_\epsilon = \sqrt{\frac{1}{M} \sum_{m=1}^{M} (\hat{d}_m - \bar{d}_m)^2}. \tag{4.18}$$

The triple-frequency combination in GPS (L1, L2, and L5) will automatically filter out all delays that are outside one chip of any of the three signals. The L5 signal has the fastest chip rate $f_{\text{chip}} = 10.23\,\text{MHz}$, so all $d > \frac{c}{f_{\text{chip}}} \approx 30\,\text{m}$ could be identified and ideally ignored, or a special multi-chip rate approach could be developed to handle them. In order to estimate the reflection delays that are smaller than ca. 30 m, the ML problem in (4.15), needs to be solved. To do this, a simple numerical solution is used, based on grid search. This means that the $P(d, \Lambda, P_{\text{LOS}}, f_n)$ surface in Fig. 4.3 is divided into steps of 1 mm along the d axis and steps of 0.1 along the Λ axis. This is followed by a numerical search for the point along the d and Λ axis that maximizes the likelihood function. This discretization results in $\Delta_d = 3000$ points along the delay axis $\Delta_\Lambda = 100$ points along the RR axis. The computational complexity is then $\mathcal{O}(\Delta_d \Delta_\Lambda)$. The signal power of the direct signal, P_{LOS}, was set to 1. A patent for this delay estimation method is pending [OB19b].

To evaluate the contribution of the prior gamma distribution, a simulation where $\Lambda = 0.8$ is held constant, with $M = 500$ Monte Carlo runs was done, once with the prior distribution and once ignoring it (Gamma($\hat{d}_m = -0.23L^2 + 5.08L - 4.08, 1) = 1$). In this simulation, for each Monte Carlo run, a number of satellites L is randomly generated between 4 and 9, then the corresponding gamma distribution shape parameter is computed according to 2.8. After this, since the root mean

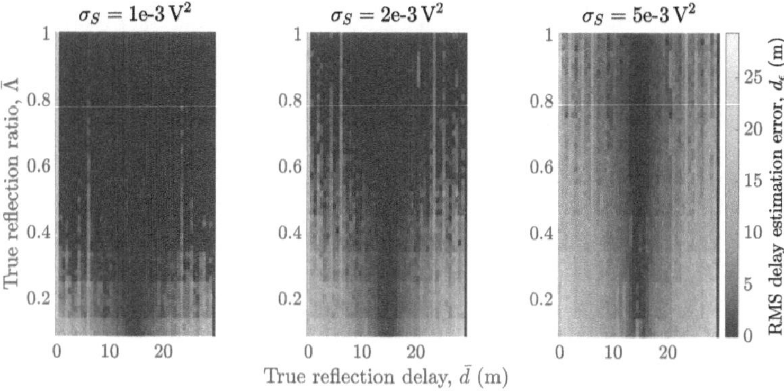

Figure 4.5: The performance of the signal power-based delay estimation highly depends on the measurement noise level. Error-free delay estimation is indicated by dark blue. The figure is adapted from [OBB20a].

square error of the model in 2.8 is approximately 0.33 m, a normal distribution error with mean 0 and standard deviation 0.33 m is added to the shape parameter. Then, a gamma distribution with this shape parameter and a scale parameter of 1 is used as a prior distribution in the reflection delay estimation. This simulation was done for 50 equally spaced measurement noise values from $1\,\mathrm{mV}^2$ to $50\,\mathrm{mV}^2$.

4.6 Results

An overview of the delay estimation for all simulated delays and RR can be found in Fig. 4.5. This is based on $M = 100$ Monte Carlo runs, using no prior distribution. It can be noted that it is more difficult to estimate the delay of weaker reflections, since they have less influence on the total received signal power. Since extremely short delays give the same interference regardless of the carrier frequency, these are almost impossible to correctly estimate. The lowest noise level ($\sigma_S \leq$ 1e-3 V^2) represents almost error-free delay estimation; under this condition most delays can be identified. However, with larger noise levels, the delay estimation is unreliable.

Next, a special case of the results from in Fig. 4.5 is presented, where Λ is kept constant at around 0.5. This is to reproduce a scenario similar to [LKR08, Fig. 6], so that a comparison with the state of the art is achieved. $M = 1000$ Monte Carlo runs were used, also without the prior gamma distribution. It is important to note that the methods presented in [LKR08] estimate the delay

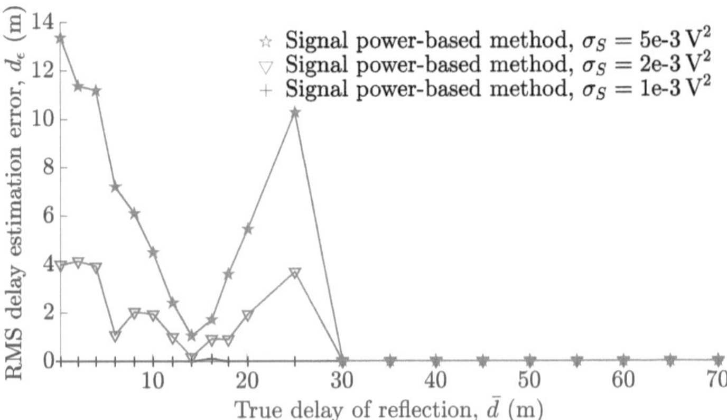

Figure 4.6: While $\sigma_S \leq 1e\text{-}3\,V^2$ the signal power-based delay estimation performs better than the state of the art ([LKR08, Fig. 6]). The figure is adapted from [OBB20a].

by sampling a high number of correlators (41) at a high rate (1 kHz). This results in a different likelihood function, and more importantly, sets high requirements on the hardware. Of the five methods presented in [LKR08, Fig. 6], three are variants of the sampling importance resampling particle filter, while two are the narrow and Strobe correlator, which are correlator methods in the delay lock loop. The results can be seen in Fig. 4.6; the condition $\sigma_S \leq 1e\text{-}3\,V^2$ is necessary for the proposed signal power-based method to perform better. As noted in Section 4.5, all delays $\bar{d} \gtrsim 30\,\mathrm{m}$ are automatically identified by the high chip rate of the L5 signal. Fig. 4.7 presents the results of the simulated to evaluate the contribution of the prior gamma distribution. As expected, it gets more difficult to correctly estimate the reflection delay with growing measurement noise, but using the prior distribution can reduce the error by several meters on average.

4.7 Discussion

Disadvantages of the proposed signal power-based delay estimation method is include that it can only handle one dominant reflection. This is the typical case in urban canyons, but in exceptional cases, two semi-strong reflections could appear, which the model does not take into account. The presented results are based only on simulations, but with a measurement noise distribution based on experiments with a real receiver, and with three different standard deviations of the measurement noise. This experiment also shows that the measurement noise is on the upper limit of what the proposed method can handle while still correctly identifying the delays, at least for the used dual-frequency receiver. This means that hardware capable of measuring signal power

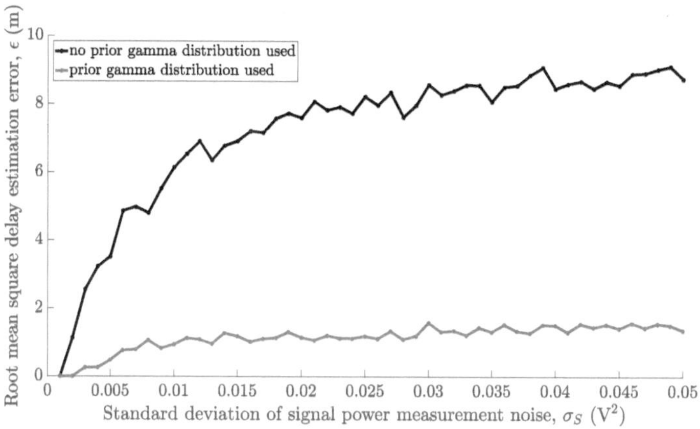

Figure 4.7: On average, the reflection delay estimation can be reduced by using the prior gamma distribution, based on the number of received satellites.

with high precision (or with high sampling rate, to filter with respect to the time) is important. The numerical solution method to the ML problem is based on grid search, which means a high computational load, however it would be easy to adapt it to other distributions of measurement noise than the Gaussian one (if another receiver would behave differently).

Advantages include that the proposed method can easily be combined with other methods, since the required signal power information is easily available (e.g., through the carrier-to-noise density ratio). In terms of hardware, the triple-frequency reception is not yet easily available in the mass-market as of 2020, but dual-frequency reception is already on its way. Greater delays are easier to identify, since the power function P_n can more easily be distinguished between the carrier frequencies when d is large (at the beginning, when d is near zero, it is almost identical for all carrier frequencies).

In both Fig. 4.5 and 4.6, a minimum delay estimation error can be found along $\bar{d} \approx 15$ m. This is because the grid search method will always end up finding one of the possible delays (from 0 m to 30 m). At 15 m, the maximum delay estimation error is then around 15 m, and since the simulation is repeated hundreds of time, this is seen as an average. However, the main message of the results is to indicate which noise levels that are acceptable for the proposed method.

In Fig. 4.6 the reflections are the same, but the compared methods are based on different input variables, requiring different types of receiver hardware, so the results should only be interpreted as a preliminary comparison. Moreover, an ML-based method is compared with a recursive method, making the comparison somewhat unfair.

4.8 Conclusions

In this chapter, we have seen that based on the signal power, an observable that is easily available on a GNSS receiver, it is possible to estimate the delay of MP reflections, to correct the resulting pseudorange errors. A triple-frequency receiver that can measure signal power with high accuracy is required for reliable performance that is better than state of the art methods. By incorporating information from a prior gamma distribution, the delay estimation becomes more robust against measurement noise. The proposed method shows good potential for combination with, e.g., advanced correlators, inertial sensors, and 3D maps.

For future work, the numerical grid-based solver needs to be improved. A solver based on, e.g., the EKF could be considered. Furthermore, other distributions of the signal power measurement noise than the Gaussian one could be studied. Finally, a dual-frequency version should be studied as an alternative to the proposed triple-frequency approach, since this would make the hardware cheaper and easier to come by.

Chapter 5

Accurate Positioning in Urban Canyons

In Chapters 2, 3 and 4, the urban canyon problem was analyzed on a per-satellite basis, and in this chapter we take the step into the position domain by combining several satellites. Specifically, the dual-frequency satellite selection method from Section 3.4 is used to minimize positioning errors in an urban canyon environment. Working in the positioning domain also allows one to combine GNSS with other sensors, such as collaborative positioning via, e.g., Wi-Fi and DR with inertial sensors, which is also done is this chapter.

The chapter is based on [OSBB20], with an extension of results for DR.

First, in Section 5.1, the problem is formulated, where the goal is to estimate the positions of one or multiple receivers with minimal error. This is done using pseudorange and SNR measurements on several frequencies, together with local ranges between receivers. Second, related work on collaborative positioning is presented in Section 5.2. Third, the an EKF positioning solution with dual-frequency satellite selection and collaborative position is introduced in Section 5.4. Fourth, Section 5.5 shows how the EKF can be supported by DR. Fifth, in Section 5.6, an urban canyon simulation is presented, together with the positioning results. Sixth, the results and the method are discussed in Section 5.7. Finally, the conclusions can be found in Section 5.8.

5.1   Problem Formulation

Since collaborative positioning is used, up to M receivers, indexed by m are considered. Their 2D positions in East, North, Up (ENU) coordinates, for each time step k, are

$$\mathbf{p}_k = \begin{bmatrix} r_k^{1,e} & r_k^{1,n} & \dots & r_k^{M,e} & r_k^{M,n} \end{bmatrix}^T. \tag{5.1}$$

Given ground truth trajectories consisting of K time steps $\bar{\mathbf{p}}_1 \dots \bar{\mathbf{p}}_K$ and the estimated trajectories

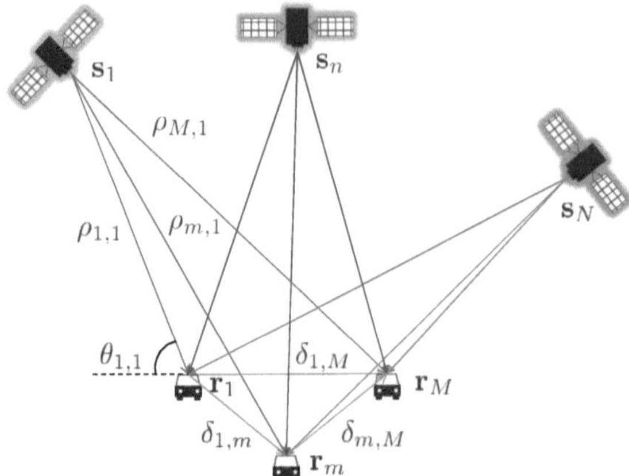

Figure 5.1: N satellites are received by M receivers, which can measure their inter-receiver distances (local ranges, δ), and share their measured pseudoranges ρ through V2V communication. The elevation of the satellite n received by the receiver m is $\theta_{m,n}$. The figure is adopted from [OSBB20], ©2020 IEEE.

$\hat{\mathbf{p}}_1 \ldots \hat{\mathbf{p}}_K$, our goal is to minimize the average positioning error

$$\epsilon = \frac{1}{K} \sum_{k=1}^{K} \sqrt{\frac{1}{2M} \left((\bar{\mathbf{p}}_k - \hat{\mathbf{p}}_k) \cdot (\bar{\mathbf{p}}_k - \hat{\mathbf{p}}_k) \right)}. \tag{5.2}$$

To do this, the following input variables are available: pseudoranges, satellite SNR, satellite positions and local ranges, see Fig. 5.1. The pseudorange measured by receiver m to satellite l on frequency 1 is

$$\rho_k^{m,l} = \sqrt{(r_k^{m,x} - s_k^{l,x})^2 + (r_k^{m,y} - s_k^{l,y})^2 + (r_k^{m,z} - s_k^{l,z})^2} + b_m + w_k^{m,l} + v_\rho, \tag{5.3}$$

where b_m is the receiver clock bias in meters, $w^{m,l}$ is the error caused by reflections (following the distributions from Section 2.9), and v_ρ is Gaussian measurement noise

$$v_\rho \sim \mathcal{N}(0, \sigma_\rho^2). \tag{5.4}$$

The variables $s_k^{l,x}$, $s_k^{l,y}$, and $s_k^{l,z}$ represent the ECEF position of the satellite l. The pseudorange is also measured on the second carrier frequency

$$\underline{\rho}_k^{m,l} = \sqrt{(r_k^{m,x} - s_k^{l,x})^2 + (r_k^{m,y} - s_k^{l,y})^2 + (r_k^{m,z} - s_k^{l,z})^2} + b_m + \underline{w}_k^{m,l} + \underline{v}_k^{m,l}, \tag{5.5}$$

where $\underline{w}_{m,l}$ is the error caused by reflections, and $\underline{v}_\rho$ is Gaussian measurement noise

$$\underline{v}_\rho \sim \mathcal{N}(0, \underline{\sigma}_\rho^2), \tag{5.6}$$

which both typically differ from the measurement errors on frequency 1.

The SNR on frequency 1 depends on the satellite elevation θ according to [DRB18]

$$S_k^{m,l} = 3.199\text{e-}5(\theta_k^{m,l})^3 - 8.1\text{e-}3(\theta_k^{m,l})^2 + 0.6613\theta_k^{m,l} + 31.38 + v_S. \tag{5.7}$$

The L2 signal is transmitted with 3 dB less power than the L1 signal

$$\underline{S}_k^{m,l} = S_k^{m,l} - 3\,\text{dB} + \underline{v}_S. \tag{5.8}$$

The SNR on both frequencies have Gaussian measurement noise

$$v_S \sim \mathcal{N}(0, \sigma_S^2) \tag{5.9}$$

$$\underline{v}_S \sim \mathcal{N}(0, \underline{\sigma}_S^2). \tag{5.10}$$

The last type of measurement is the local ranges, which are distances between two receivers m and m_*

$$\delta_k^{m,m_*} = \|\mathbf{r}_k^m - \mathbf{r}_k^{m_*}\| + v_\delta, \tag{5.11}$$

that have Gaussian measurement noise

$$v_\delta \sim \mathcal{N}(0, \sigma_\delta^2). \tag{5.12}$$

The local ranges could be measured by, e.g., lidar, radar or the strength of the communication channel, which decides the variance of the measurement noise, σ_δ^2.

5.2 Related Work

For this chapter, related work in two areas is relevant: multi-frequency signal processing methods and collaborative positioning.

Multi-Frequency Detection and Mitigation of Reflections Multi-frequency GNSS signal processing can be used to detect and mitigate errors in urban canyons, based on, e.g., SNR [SG16].

More detailed related work on multi-frequency signal processing methods can be found in Section 1.3 and in Chapters 3 and 4.

Collaborative Positioning V2V and Vehicle to Infrastructure Communication (V2I) are two emerging technologies that allow vehicles to communicate with each other, and with infrastructure (such as traffic lights), respectively. With V2V, vehicles can exchange GNSS data such as pseudorange measurements. V2V for collaborative positioning has been extensively studied, on one hand to achieve more accurate positioning in open areas [MNH15, AD13, SMM+14, CSGS10]. More specifically, [MNH15] proposes the angle approximation method and absolute sum of double differencing approach, so that the most accurated pseudoranges can be selected. A discussion of the accuracy provided by cooperative positioning can be found in [AD13], while [SMM+14] discusses cooperative positiong based on RTK. A hybrid cooperative UKF that fuses both satellites and terrestrial receivers is presented in [CSGS10]. Furthermore, V2V for collaborative positioning can be used to improve positioning in urban areas [PCW10, OSM+12, ZWH18, SKD16, KKK15, JCDJ14, Ala11]. The Cramér-Rao bound for hybrid cooperative positioning was derived by [PCW10]. An approach that combines GNSS, SBAS, V2V with and advanced map matching can be found in [OSM+12]. An approach based on consistency checks between several vehicles was presented by [ZWH18]. The Nav2Nav solution uses machine learning to detect NLOS [SKD16]. Two technies were prosed by [KKK15]: the multipath-resistant hybrid sum–product algorithm over a wireless network and the multipath-resistant hybrid cooperative extended Kalman filter. The Wilcoxon method to detect reflections, combined with a Vehicular Ad-hoc Network can be found in [JCDJ14]. The work [Ala11] presents a a cooperative positioning that reduces the number of required satellites to two. In addition to communicating, the distances between the communicating vehicles can be measured. This is called the local range, and can be based on, e.g., the strength of the communication signal, radar, or lidar. The main advantage of collaborative positioning in urban areas is that nearby receivers will obtain different reflection errors from the same satellite, since the received reflections highly depend on the receiver position. Moreover, nearby receivers might receive different satellites, and by communicating their measurements, the number of available satellite measurements are increased. Finally, the local ranges make even more measurements available.

5.3 Gauss-Newton

For comparison purposes, the GN [Bjö96] method is used. It is often used to solve the multilateration problem of the GPS navigation equations, since it can solve non-linear equation systems. In the equation system, there are four unknown variables per receiver

$$\mathbf{x} = [r^{1,x} \quad r^{1,y} \quad r^{1,z} \quad b^1 \cdots r^{M,x} \quad r^{M,y} \quad r^{M,z} \quad b^M]^T. \tag{5.13}$$

There are two conditions that can stop the GN solver:

- if the solution is below the tolerance, set to 1e-6, or

- when more than 100 iterations are done.

More details on the GN solver are given in Section 1.2. The GN solver includes no transition model, so no assumption of the movement of the vehicles can support the position estimation. If less than four satellites are received, the solver will exceed the maximal number of iterations and end up without a solution. The GN solver was modified in two ways. First, for a new time step, it uses the solution of the previous time step as initial solution, for improved speed and stability. Second, it uses the reference position as a solution for the first two time steps, so that the solver is initially stable. In general, the GN solver is less sensitive to divergence than the EKF, which however possesses other advantages.

5.4 Extended Kalman Filter for Collaborative Positioning

The EKF is a common tool to estimate the position of a receiver based on GNSS measurements, and it can be further developed to also include pseudorange measurements from other receivers, along with local range measurements, as will be done here. The local range measurements are then treated as pseudorange measurements with no clock bias, and the position of the other receiver is replacing the satellite position. The EKF is a an extension of the Kalman filter [Kal60], where a linearization through Taylor approximation is made. The basic version of the EKF for GNSS is explained in Section 1.2, here it will be extended to work with collaborative positioning and dual-frequency measurements. It incorporates a transition model, which assumes how the receivers move between two time steps. A simple but effective approach is the CV transition model, where the velocities of the receivers are assumed to stay constant. For this, the state space includes the 3D position (which is desired), the clock bias, and also their derivatives for all receivers

$$\mathbf{x}_k = [r_k^{1,x} \quad \dot{r}_k^{1,x} \quad r_k^{1,y} \quad \dot{r}_k^{1,y} \quad r_k^{1,z} \quad \dot{r}_k^{1,z} \quad b_k^1 \quad \dot{b}_k^1 \quad \cdots$$
$$r_k^{M,x} \quad \dot{r}_k^{M,x} \quad r_k^{M,y} \quad \dot{r}_k^{M,y} \quad r_k^{M,z} \quad \dot{r}_k^{M,z} \quad b_k^M \quad \dot{b}_k^M]^T. \quad (5.14)$$

The transition matrix is the relation between the current state and its previous state

$$\mathbf{A} = \mathbf{I}_{4M} \otimes \begin{bmatrix} 1 & \tau \\ 0 & 1 \end{bmatrix}, \quad (5.15)$$

where τ is the sampling interval and $\otimes$ is the Kronecker product [Bro06]. $\mathbf{I}_d$ is an identity matrix of dimension d.

The process covariance matrix for the x, y, and z positions is

$$\mathbf{Q}_{xyz} = \sigma_{xyz}^2 \begin{bmatrix} \frac{\tau^3}{3} & \frac{\tau^2}{2} \\ \frac{\tau^2}{2} & \tau \end{bmatrix}, \tag{5.16}$$

and for the clock bias and its drift it is

$$\mathbf{Q}_b = \begin{bmatrix} S_f \tau + S_g \frac{\tau^3}{3} & \frac{S_g \tau^2}{2} \\ \frac{S_g \tau^2}{2} & S_g \tau \end{bmatrix}. \tag{5.17}$$

Together, they form the process covariance matrix for one receiver m

$$\mathbf{Q}_m = \mathrm{diag}\left(\begin{bmatrix} \mathbf{Q}_{xyz} & \mathbf{Q}_{xyz} & \mathbf{Q}_{xyz} & \mathbf{Q}_b \end{bmatrix} \right). \tag{5.18}$$

To create a diagonal matrix with a vector input as its diagonal, the function $\mathrm{diag}(\cdot)$ i used

$$\mathrm{diag}\left(\begin{bmatrix} a_1 & a_2 & a_3 \end{bmatrix} \right) = \begin{bmatrix} a_1 & 0 & 0 \\ 0 & a_2 & 0 \\ 0 & 0 & a_3 \end{bmatrix}. \tag{5.19}$$

By repeating $\mathbf{Q}_m$ m times in the diagonal, the $8M \times 8M$ complete process covariance matrix is created

$$\mathbf{Q} = \mathbf{I}_M \otimes \mathbf{Q}_m. \tag{5.20}$$

The error covariance matrix is diagonal and of dimension $8M \times 8M$. It is initialized according to

$$\mathbf{P}_{k-1} = \mathbf{I}_{8M} \otimes p_0, \tag{5.21}$$

where p_0 is a tuning parameter, with the value given in Table 5.1.

Furthermore, an initial estimate of the state, $\hat{\mathbf{x}}_{k-1}^-$, is needed. In an urban scenario, an accurate initial state is difficult to compute, which can cause the EKF to diverge. For this reason, the reference position is used for the first two time time steps.

When the initial values are set, the EKF starts a loop, where first a prediction of the state covariance

$$\hat{\mathbf{x}}^- = \mathbf{A}\hat{\mathbf{x}}_{k-1}, \tag{5.22}$$

and the error covariance

$$\mathbf{P}_k^- = \mathbf{A}\mathbf{P}_{k-1}\mathbf{A}^T + \mathbf{Q}, \tag{5.23}$$

is made.

Subsequently, for each receiver m, I_m satellites indexed by i_m are selected using Algorithm 2. Next, the linearization by the Jacobian measurement matrix is done

$$\mathbf{J}_{m,\rho} = \begin{bmatrix} \frac{\partial \rho_{m,1}}{\partial x} & 0 & \frac{\partial \rho_{m,1}}{\partial y} & 0 & \frac{\partial \rho_{m,1}}{\partial z} & 0 & 1 & 0 \\ \vdots & \vdots & \vdots & \vdots & \vdots & \vdots & \vdots & \vdots \\ \frac{\partial \rho_{m,I_m}}{\partial x} & 0 & \frac{\partial \rho_{m,I_m}}{\partial y} & 0 & \frac{\partial \rho_{m,I_m}}{\partial z} & 0 & 1 & 0 \\ \frac{\partial \rho_{m,1}}{\partial x} & 0 & \frac{\partial \rho_{m,1}}{\partial y} & 0 & \frac{\partial \rho_{m,1}}{\partial z} & 0 & 1 & 0 \\ \vdots & \vdots & \vdots & \vdots & \vdots & \vdots & \vdots & \vdots \\ \frac{\partial \rho_{m,I_m}}{\partial x} & 0 & \frac{\partial \rho_{m,I_m}}{\partial y} & 0 & \frac{\partial \rho_{m,I_m}}{\partial z} & 0 & 1 & 0 \end{bmatrix}, \tag{5.24}$$

where

$$\frac{\partial \rho_{m,i_m}}{\partial x} = \frac{-(s^{i_m,x} - \hat{r}^{m,x})}{\sqrt{(s^{i_m,x} - \hat{r}^{m,x})^2 + (s^{i_m,y} - \hat{r}^{m,y})^2 + (s^{i_m,z} - \hat{r}^{m,z})^2}} \tag{5.25}$$

$$\frac{\partial \rho_{m,i_m}}{\partial y} = \frac{-(s^{i_m,y} - \hat{r}^{m,y})}{\sqrt{(s^{i_m,x} - \hat{r}^{m,x})^2 + (s^{i_m,y} - \hat{r}^{m,y})^2 + (s^{i_m,z} - \hat{r}^{m,z})^2}} \tag{5.26}$$

$$\frac{\partial \rho_{m,i_m}}{\partial z} = \frac{-(s^{i_m,z} - \hat{r}^{m,z})}{\sqrt{(s^{i_m,x} - \hat{r}^{m,x})^2 + (s^{i_m,y} - \hat{r}^{m,y})^2 + (s^{i_m,z} - \hat{r}^{m,z})^2}}. \tag{5.27}$$

Each row appears twice for each receiver, since there are two pseudorange measurements (one per frequency).

Between all M receivers, there can be up to $\Xi = M^2 - M$ local range measurements, indexed by ξ. The Jacobian for the local range measurement between two receivers m_1 and m_2 is

$$\mathbf{J}_{\xi,\delta} = \begin{bmatrix} \frac{\partial \delta^{m,m_*}}{\partial x} & 0 & \frac{\partial \delta^{m,m_*}}{\partial y} & 0 & \frac{\partial \delta^{m,m_*}}{\partial z} & 0 & 0 & 0 \end{bmatrix}, \tag{5.28}$$

where

$$\frac{\partial \delta^{m,m_*}}{\partial x} = \frac{-(\hat{r}^{m_*,x} - \hat{r}^{m,x})}{\sqrt{(\hat{r}^{m_*,x} - \hat{r}^{m,x})^2 + (\hat{r}^{m_*,y} - \hat{r}^{m,y})^2 + (\hat{r}^{m_*,z} - \hat{r}^{m,z})^2}} \tag{5.29}$$

$$\frac{\partial \delta^{m,m_*}}{\partial y} = \frac{-(\hat{r}^{m_*,y} - \hat{r}^{m,y})}{\sqrt{(\hat{r}^{m_*,x} - \hat{r}^{m,x})^2 + (\hat{r}^{m_*,y} - \hat{r}^{m,y})^2 + (\hat{r}^{m_*,z} - \hat{r}^{m,z})^2}} \tag{5.30}$$

$$\frac{\partial \delta^{m,m_*}}{\partial z} = \frac{-(\hat{r}^{m_*,z} - \hat{r}^{m,z})}{\sqrt{(\hat{r}^{m_*,x} - \hat{r}^{m,x})^2 + (\hat{r}^{m_*,y} - \hat{r}^{m,y})^2 + (\hat{r}^{m_*,z} - \hat{r}^{m,z})^2}}, \tag{5.31}$$

The complete Jacobian for all measurements and all M receivers then becomes

$$\mathbf{J} = \begin{bmatrix} \mathbf{J}_{1,\rho} & \mathbf{0}_{2I_m \times 8} & \cdots & & \cdots & \mathbf{0}_{2I_m \times 8} \\ & & \ddots & & & \\ \mathbf{0}_{2I_m \times 8} & \mathbf{J}_{m,\rho} & \cdots & & \cdots & \mathbf{0}_{2I_m \times 8} \\ & & & \ddots & & \\ \mathbf{0}_{2I_m \times 8} & \cdots & \cdots & \mathbf{0}_{2I_m \times 8} & \mathbf{J}_{M,\rho} \\ \mathbf{J}_{1,\delta} & \mathbf{0}_{1 \times 8} & \cdots & & \cdots & \mathbf{0}_{1 \times 8} \\ \mathbf{0}_{1 \times 8} & \ddots & & & & \vdots \\ \vdots & & \cdots & \mathbf{J}_{\xi,\delta} & \cdots & & \vdots \\ \vdots & & & & \ddots & \mathbf{0}_{1 \times 8} \\ \mathbf{0}_{1 \times 8} & \cdots & & \cdots & \mathbf{0}_{1 \times 8} & \mathbf{J}_{\Xi,\delta} \end{bmatrix}, \tag{5.32}$$

where $\mathbf{0}_{\text{rows} \times \text{columns}}$ is a rows $\times$ columns-dimensional zero matrix.

The measurement error auto-covariance matrix

$$\mathbf{R} = \mathrm{diag}\left(\begin{bmatrix} \mathbf{R}_{1,\rho} & \cdots & \mathbf{R}_{m,\rho} & \cdots & \mathbf{R}_{M,\rho} & \mathbf{R}_{\delta} \end{bmatrix} \right), \tag{5.33}$$

is a diagonal matrix, with the pseudorange measurement variance of frequency 1, followed by the pseudorange measurement variance of frequency 2, repeated for each receiver

$$\mathbf{R}_{m,\rho} = [\underbrace{\sigma_1^2 \quad \cdots \quad \sigma_1^2}_{I_m \text{ times}} \underbrace{\sigma_\rho^2 \quad \cdots \quad \sigma_\rho^2}_{I_m \text{ times}}], \tag{5.34}$$

ending with the pseudorange measurement variance of the local ranges

$$\mathbf{R}_{\delta} = \begin{bmatrix} \underbrace{\sigma_\delta^2 \quad \cdots \quad \sigma_\delta^2}_{\Xi \text{ times}} \end{bmatrix}. \tag{5.35}$$

Then, the Kalman gain

$$\mathbf{K} = \mathbf{P}_k^- \mathbf{J}^T (\mathbf{J}\mathbf{P}_k^- \mathbf{J}^T + \mathbf{R})^{-1}, \tag{5.36}$$

is computed.

The dual-frequency pseudoranges of both frequencies from each receiver, and all local range measurements form together the measurement vector

$$\mathbf{z} = \begin{bmatrix} \mathbf{z}_\rho \\ \mathbf{z}_\delta \end{bmatrix}, \tag{5.37}$$

where the pseudoranges are

$$
\begin{aligned}
\mathbf{z}_\rho = [\rho^{1,1} \quad \cdots \quad \rho^{1,I_1} \quad \underline{\rho}^{1,1} \quad \cdots \quad \underline{\rho}^{1,I_1} \quad \cdots \\
\rho^{m,1} \quad \cdots \quad \rho^{m,I_m} \quad \underline{\rho}^{m,1} \quad \cdots \quad \underline{\rho}^{m,I_m} \quad \cdots \\
\rho^{M,1} \quad \cdots \quad \rho^{M,I_M} \quad \underline{\rho}^{M,1} \quad \cdots \quad \underline{\rho}^{M,I_M}]^T.
\end{aligned}
\tag{5.38}
$$

and the local ranges are

$$
\mathbf{z}_\delta = \begin{bmatrix} \delta_1 & \cdots & \delta_\Xi \end{bmatrix}^T.
\tag{5.39}
$$

Thereafter, the current state estimate is given by

$$
\hat{\mathbf{x}}_k = \hat{\mathbf{x}}^- + \mathbf{K}(\mathbf{z} - \mathbf{J}\hat{\mathbf{x}}^-).
\tag{5.40}
$$

Subsequently, an update of the error covariance matrix is performed

$$
\mathbf{P}_k = \mathbf{P}_k^- - \mathbf{K}\mathbf{J}\mathbf{P}_k^-.
\tag{5.41}
$$

Finally, the EKF processes the next time step by restarting from (5.22).

5.5 Positioning with Dead-Reckoning

Low-cost Microelectromechanical System (MEMS) sensors can support satellite navigation by providing measurements that are always available at a high sample rate. For automotive applications, a typical combination is a gyroscope measuring angular rates in one to three dimensions and a wheel odometer that counts driven distance. A simple approach for DR is to measurement only the yaw angular rate

$$
\Omega_k^m = \frac{\psi_k - \psi_{k-1}}{\tau} + v_\Omega,
\tag{5.42}
$$

with Gaussian measurement noise

$$
v_\Omega \sim \mathcal{N}(0, \sigma_\Omega^2).
\tag{5.43}
$$

The main problem of this measurement is that the measurement error will accumulate and grow with time due to the integration (to get an angle from the angular rate measurement), which means that it is not reliable by itself, if used for a long time. In reality, the mean of the noise is not zero, due to the zero-point offset of the gyroscope. This is typically compensated by detecting when the vehicle is not moving, and saving the offset in a table for several temperatures (since this offset depends on temperature).

The odometer gives distance measurements and the speed can be determined by

$$D_k^m = \|\mathbf{r}_k^m - \mathbf{r}_{k-1}^m\| + v_D,$$
(5.44)

where

$$v_D \sim \mathcal{N}(0, \sigma_D^2).$$
(5.45)

As for the gyroscope, the mean of the odometer noise is in reality non-zero, due to a scale point offset. This is compensated by measuring the tire temperature and pressure. Furthermore, if the odometer readings are transmitted via Controller Area Network (CAN), they typically arrive with irregular delays, causing further problems.

The estimated velocity in east-north coordinates according to the gyroscope and odometer is then

$$\dot{\mathbf{r}}_{\mathrm{DR}} = \begin{bmatrix} \|\dot{\mathbf{r}}_k\| \cos(\psi_k) \\ \|\dot{\mathbf{r}}_k\| \sin(\psi_k) \\ 0 \end{bmatrix},$$
(5.46)

while it is according to GNSS

$$\dot{\mathbf{r}}_{\mathrm{GNSS}} = \mathbf{T}_{\mathrm{ECEF}\rightarrow\mathrm{ENU}}\left(\hat{\mathbf{r}}_k\right) - \mathbf{T}_{\mathrm{ECEF}\rightarrow\mathrm{ENU}}\left(\hat{\mathbf{r}}_{k-1}\right),$$
(5.47)

where $\mathbf{T}_{\mathrm{ECEF}\rightarrow\mathrm{ENU}}$ is the ECEF to ENU conversion matrix given in [KH07, p. 29].

The velocities based on GNSS and DR are combined

$$\hat{\mathbf{r}}_k = \hat{\mathbf{r}}_{k-1} + (\chi \dot{\mathbf{r}}_{\mathrm{GNSS}} + (1 - \chi)\dot{\mathbf{r}}_{\mathrm{DR}})\tau,$$
(5.48)

with the weight being based on the EKF covariance

$$\chi = \begin{cases} \frac{15}{\|\mathbf{P}_k\|}, & \text{if } \frac{15}{\|\mathbf{P}_k\|} \leq 1 \\ 1, & \text{otherwise} \end{cases}.$$
(5.49)

The logic behind this weighting rule is that GNSS-based EKF covariance will increase when reflections are present, thus the DR-based position is weighted more heavily.

5.6   Simulation

To evaluate the performance of the proposed positioning methods, a simulation with two environments was setup, where $M = 4$ vehicles are moving in a rounded square pattern. The first environment is open-sky, where all satellites above $10°$ elevation are received. The second environment was generated according to Chapter 2, with the same ray tracing functionality to

Table 5.1: The following values were used in the simulation and to tune the EKF.

Notation	Description	Value
	Simulation parameters	
τ	time interval	1 s
σ_ρ	pseudorange measurement standard deviation f_1	0.1 m
$\underline{\sigma}_\rho$	pseudorange measurement standard deviation f_2	0.1 m
σ_S	SNR measurement standard deviation f_1	1 dB
$\underline{\sigma}_S$	SNR measurement standard deviation f_2	1 dB
σ_δ	local range measurement standard deviation	0.1 m
σ_{xyz}	x, y, and z position standard deviation	1 m
σ_Ω	gyroscope heading rate measurement standard deviation	0.1 rad/s
σ_D	odometer standard deviation	0.001 m
S_g	clock bias covariance	0.1 m^2
S_f	clock bias drift covariance	36 m$^2 \cdot$ s^{-2}
p_0	initial error covariance	0.01 m^2
	EKF tuning	
σ_ρ	pseudorange measurement standard deviation f_1	1.5 m
$\underline{\sigma}_\rho$	pseudorange measurement standard deviation f_2	1.5 m
σ_δ	local range measurement standard deviation	0.1 m

generate reflections. The middle block was removed, creating an open square that allows an unobstructed V2V channel, see Fig. 5.2. The heights of these buildings follow a Rice distribution with a non-centrality parameter of 35 m and a spread of 5 m. Each building block side consists of five buildings with a width of 11 m. The road width is 20 m. A multi-constellation approach was used, with 31 GPS and 24 Galileo satellites, all sharing the same clock bias. All receivers use a correlator with 3 points, spaced half a chip apart, see Section 2.9 for more details on the receiver simulation. The same trajectory (based on [SKJF19,SLM20]) was repeated and averaged over 1000 Monte Carlo runs, to account for different realizations of the measurement noise. Table 5.1 gives detail on the tuning of the EKF and the simulation parameters. The pseudorange measurement standard deviations σ_ρ and $\underline{\sigma}_\rho$ are tuned to a higher value than the simulated one, to account for MP and NLOS errors in addition to the Gaussian noise.

Gauss-Newton Versus Extended Kalman Filter The first part of the results compares the GN solver with EKF, without yet including the DR results. The results are visualized upon the reference trajectories, with the Circular Error Probable (CEP) at 50% averaged over all Monte Carlo runs, in Fig. 5.3 and 5.4. In the open area, see Fig. 5.3, the disadvantage of using a CV with the EKF can be seen. Since the vehicle velocity is not constant while turning, the errors are larger just after turning. This is not the case for GN, since no transition model is used. In the urban area, see Fig.5.4, the disadvantage of GN can be seen, where the pseudorange errors cause the solver to find a local minimum in some areas, where the reflection situation is particularly problematic. The

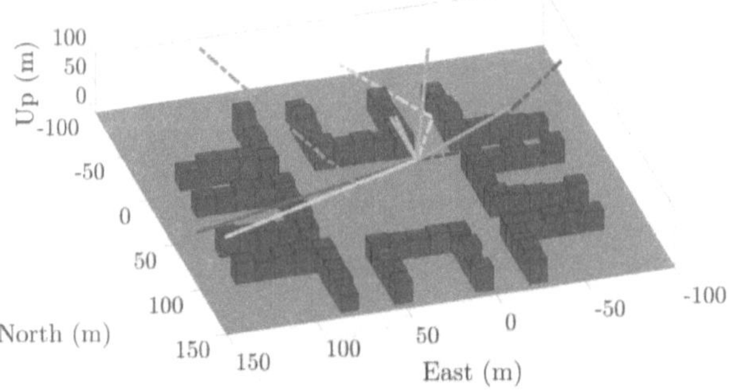

Figure 5.2: In the urban square, reflections (dashed) and line-of-sight signals (solid) are present. The figure is adopted from [OSBB20], ©2020 IEEE.

dual-frequency collaborative EKF, however, manages to keep the error low, even in the urban area.

Extended Kalman Filter and Dead-Reckoning A summary of all positioning results for the EKF can be found in Tables 5.2 and 5.3, the dual-frequency collaborative dead-reckoning position solution works well in both environments. In the open environment, the errors generally stay

Table 5.2: Positioning results in the open environment.

mean 2D error, ϵ (m)	$M = 1$	$M = 4$
1-frequency	0.23 0.23 (DR)	0.16 0.16 (DR)
2-frequency	0.56 0.56 (DR)	0.29 0.29 (DR)

Table 5.3: Positioning results in the urban environment.

mean 2D error, ϵ (m)	$M = 1$	$M = 4$
1-frequency	24.9 25.0 (DR)	41.2 40.5 (DR)
2-frequency	6.79 5.64 (DR)	2.46 2.32 (DR)

under 1 m, the only problematic case is the dual frequency non-collaborative positioning filter, which shows errors up to 3 m (see Fig. 5.5 and Fig. 5.6). There are two reasons for this: firstly, when

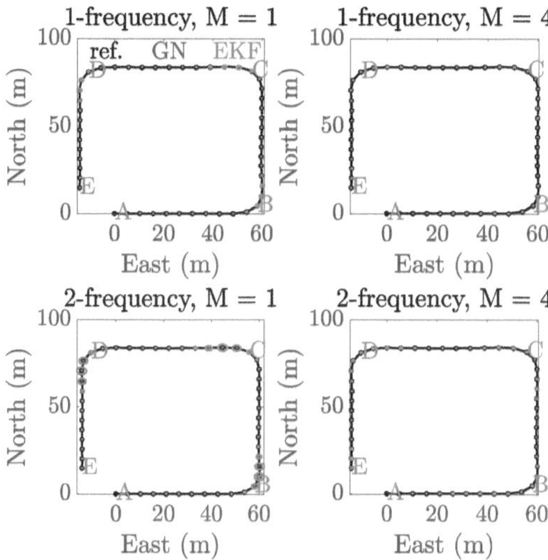

Figure 5.3: In the open area, the positioning is mainly problem-free, except for the Constant Velocity (CV) transition model of the Extended Kalman Filter (EKF), which is error-prone where the vehicle is turning.

the vehicle is turning the CV model contradicts the dynamics, introducing errors there. Secondly, the dual-frequency satellite selection algorithm removes too many satellites, and without local ranges to compensate for these, another error is introduced. In the urban environment, large errors are introduced, especially when no dual-frequency satellite selection is used, see Fig. 5.7 and Fig. 5.8. The combination of dual-frequency satellite selection and collaborative positioning succeeds in reducing the average error to a few meters. DR reduces the error slightly further in some critical areas.

5.7 Discussion

We have seen that in spite of the assumption of Gaussian measurement noise of an EKF, it can still work well for positioning, even in urban areas. For this, the measurements need to be filtered before being used in the EKF so the most erroneous ones are excluded. This pushes the error distribution of the used measurements to a more Gaussian one. Otherwise, the positioning error can increase to values of up to 50 m in just 1 second. The advantages of DR are mainly observed in specific situations (such as a deep urban canyon or a tunnel), but when performing satellite

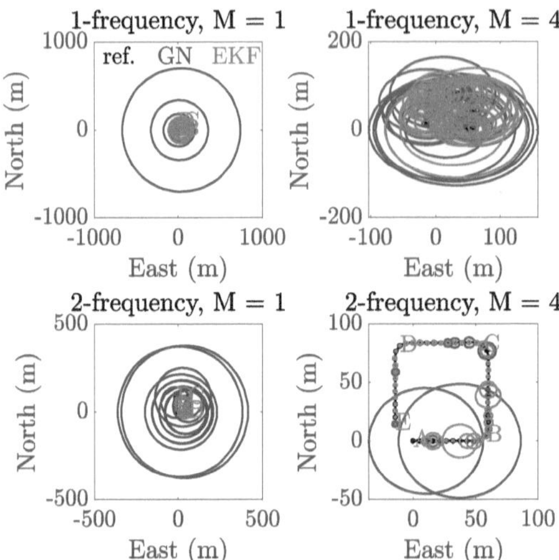

Figure 5.4: In the urban area, the Gauss-Newton (GN) solver finds many solutions that are wrong by hundreds of meters due to pseudorange errors. The dual-frequency collaborative Extended Kalman Filter (EKF), however, manages to keep the positioning errors to a few meters most of the time.

selection and averaging over many simulations, the advantage becomes less clear.

The results in this chapter are not based on real satellite data or data from GNSS signal generators, but they are only based on simulations. Realistic noise is however used on all simulated measurements, and the pseudoranges have reflection errors based on a 3D city environment with ray tracing. Furthermore, the results have been compared with a reference reflection-free scenario, to make sure that the positioning algorithm is not suitable only to urban areas; the open areas have to still work well.

5.8   Conclusions

In this chapter, we have seen how positioning errors in a challenging urban environment can be reduced by combining two complementary technologies. Collaborative positioning provides more measurements (in terms of pseudoranges of other vehicles and local ranges), while dual-frequency observables removes reflection-affected satellite measurements. A collaborative positioning EKF capable of combining dual-frequency pseudorange measurements and local range measurements

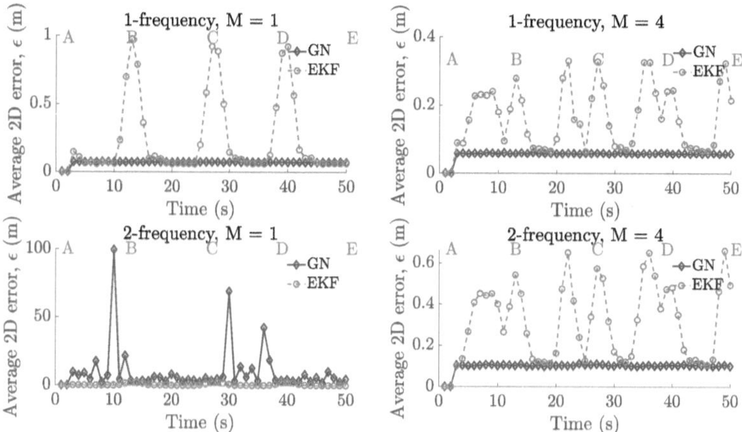

Figure 5.5: In an open environment, positioning errors are generally low, however dual-frequency satellite selection unsupported by collaborative positioning does not work very well. The magenta markers ABCDE correspond the locations specified in Fig. 5.3.

has been proposed, reducing the average positioning error to a couple of meters. With the addition of a simple DR solution with a gyroscope and an odometer, the errors can be reduced slightly more. Even though the EKF is suboptimal for handling the non-Gaussian measurement errors caused by reflections, a dual-frequency based filtering of the erroneous measurements shows promising results.

A natural next step would be to implement a positioning solution based on, e.g., the particle filter or the UKF instead of the EKF. These could handle the non-Gaussian errors better. One could also integrate the satellite selection step with the EKF, by adapting the covariance of the measurements based on the dual-frequency observables, instead of the current binary choice solution. In this work, the position accuracy has been the focus, however in the future states such as heading and velocity could also be considered.

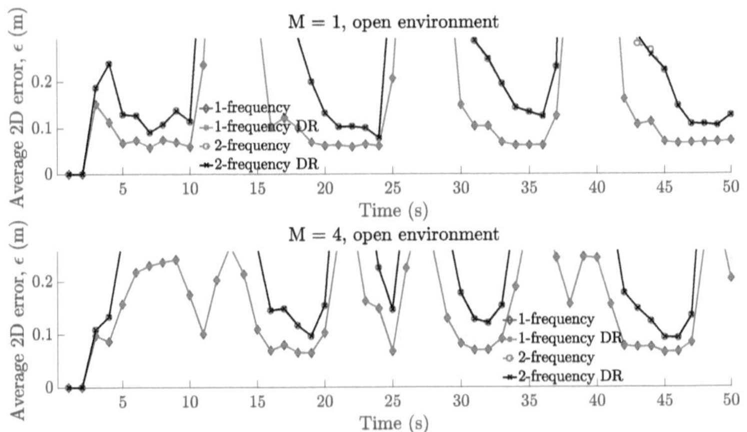

Figure 5.6: When zooming in on the results from Fig. 5.5, one can see that the Dead Reckoning (DR) makes little difference in an open environment.

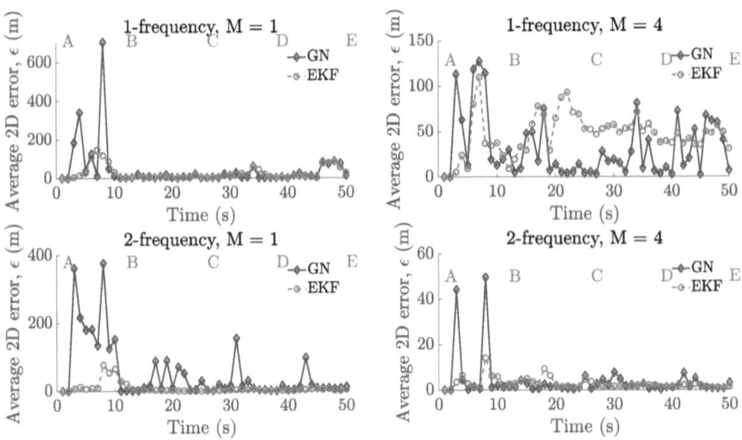

Figure 5.7: The urban environment is problematic for positioning, but the errors can be reduced to a few meters by combining dual-frequency satellite selection and collaborative positioning. The magenta markers ABCDE correspond the locations specified in Fig. 5.4.

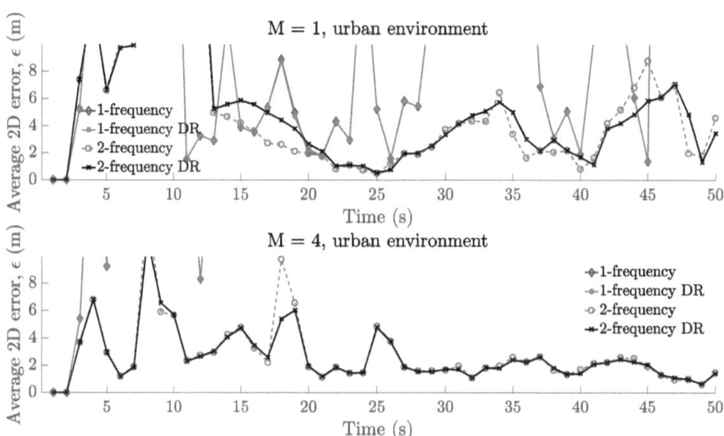

Figure 5.8: A zoom of Fig. 5.7 shows that the dual-frequency collaborative Dead Reckoning (DR) is especially helpful during certain time steps.

Chapter 6

Conclusions

In this chapter, the conclusions of this book are summarized. This book has shown that there is a lot of potential in dual and triple-frequency receivers to improve positioning in urban canyons, by excluding the most erroneous satellites, by correcting their measurements, or by combining multi-frequency GNSS with other sensors. These are examples of different approaches that all profit from multi-frequency in different ways.

We have seen that a ray tracing simulation is a powerful tool to get a better understanding of satellite navigation problems in urban areas. This is especially true to relate the building height to the seriousness of the problems, since this parameter is hard to variate in real life. Furthermore, we can conclude that GNSS positioning in urban areas is a challenging problem, because the pseudorange errors caused by reflections follow a highly non-Gaussian distribution. These errors have a strong linear correlation between them on two frequencies in the case of NLOS reception. MP, however, causes in general smaller and more unpredictable errors. A simple second-degree polynomial taking the number of satellites as input can give important information about the reflection delay distribution, which can be approximated as a gamma distribution.

Furthermore, if measurements of pseudorange, SNR, or correlator output are available on several carrier frequencies, the received satellites can be classified according to their reception mode, and ranked within each reception mode. This is possible, mainly since the interference between direct signal and reflection causes variations in the SNR and correlation power in case of MP. Thus, a satellite combination that reduces the positioning can be achieved using simple white-box thumb rules with low computational complexity. This shows promising results in a preliminary validation during a test drive with real satellite data as well.

When satellite selection is problematic due to a lack of satellites with a low measurement error, their measurements can be corrected and still used. This can be done for MP satellites when the signal power (or a closely related variable) is available on several carrier frequencies, by exploiting the fact that MP causes interference between the direct signal and the reflection, which is visible in the signal power. By solving an ML problem, the reflection delay of each satellite can be estimated, which in combination with an inverse MP error envelope can correct the pseudorange measurement. In this way, positioning in areas with few satellites and significant MP reception can be improved.

Finally, GNSS is especially useful in combination with complementary sensors (such as other wireless signals and IMU). We have seen that, in particular the previously mentioned dual-frequency satellite selection methods, in combination with collaborative positioning and DR can significantly reduce positioning errors in urban areas, in comparison with stand-alone GNSS that naively uses all satellite measurements. Despite the non-Gaussian measurement errors on the pseudoranges, the EKF is a good positioning algorithm when combining different sensors, especially when supported by efficient satellite selection. According to the simulation, the EKF solution that combines collaborative positioning with dual-frequency satellite selection and DR can reduce the positioning errors in difficult areas to a couple of meters.

Outlook This book has focused on dual-frequency receivers. These are closer to the mass-market, however triple-frequency receivers are also of interest. In the future, a thorough comparison of the proposed methods in their dual- and triple-frequency version should be done. Furthermore, the methods could use more validation with real satellite data, with high-quality ground truth data that can record reflections with high precision, using, e.g., multi-correlator hardware.

There is a need for standardization of reflection scenarios, so that novel methods can be easily compared. A public data set with a maximum amount of parameters and precise reference data on the reflections is needed, or a simulation that generates a realistic scenario can be used. The method and the code from Chapter 2 can be used as a basis for the latter suggestion, so that identical reflection scenarios can be used to validate and compare multiple MP mitigation methods.

The performance of the satellite selection problem could possibly be improved with machine learning, especially if many satellites and parameters at a high sampling rate are available. In general, there is little research on machine learning for GNSS problems, and for well-defined sub-problems there is great potential for this. Especially simpler algorithms, such as naive Bayes classification and decision trees would be of interest.

The delay estimation in Chapter 4 could be significantly improved by finding a more efficient solution to the ML problem, such as a GN solver or an iterative EKF. Also here, the trade-off between a dual and triple-frequency approach should be studied. Depending on the receiver, the ML problem could be also derived for non-Gaussian signal power measurement noise distributions.

The platform sensor fusion approach presented in Chapter 5 could be extended to including more visual sensors (such as lidar) and 3D maps. This would give an idea of how much these additional information sources can further reduce positioning errors in urban areas. A thorough comparison of the possibility to reduce reflection errors of all these technologies would be useful, so that a good trade-off between error reduction capacity and price can be made, to find an optimal combination for each use case and budget.

To sum up, the positioning in urban areas becomes less of a problem as the number of high-quality sensors increases. However, designing a robust urban canyon positioning solution that is based solely on low-cost GNSS is still major challenge, but multi-frequency receivers are a promising approach to this.

Appendix A

Simulation Source Code

The MATLAB source code of the urban canyon simulation that is used in Chapters 2 and 5 is available at `https://github.com/Fusion-Goettingen`. Most parameters can be manually changed, so one can create a custom reflection scenario, or reproduce the results presented in this book. The satellite orbits were generated using the function "Satellite Constellation" [S. 18] (modified to support a custom sampling time and a custom start time of the day to allow fast-forwarding of the satellite constellation). The satellite ranging codes are based on [Dan19].

www.ingramcontent.com/pod-product-compliance
Lightning Source LLC
LaVergne TN
LVHW041728190726
843493LV00007B/2256